Overcoming
AWkward

Title: Overcoming Awkward: The Introvert's Guide
to Networking, Marketing, and Sales
By: Monica Parkin
Edited by: Angee Costa
Cover Design: 846 Publishing
Copyright 2021

Permission: For information on getting permission for reprints and excerpts, contact:

Monica Parkin: mortgages@monicaparkin.ca

Acknowledgements

For years, I wanted to write a book but thought that, as a person with ADHD, I would be unable to focus on the task long enough to complete a project of this magnitude. But when I saw a 30-day book writing challenge advertised, I gained the confidence to try it.

Thank you to my oldest daughter who said without hesitation, "Mom you can probably actually do this. A month is the perfect amount of time for you to stay focused on one thing;" and to my son who said, "You are experiencing a phenomenon called hyper-fixation. It won't last long, so take advantage of it before a new project catches your attention." Also, to my very patient husband and youngest daughter who gave up many movie nights so I could work on this late into the evenings. Thank you, Mom and Dad, for always being my biggest cheerleaders and my bestie, Kristina, for loving authentic, quirky me before I did ☺.

Huge thanks to my amazing editor who took my long run-on chapters and organized them into smaller more succinct chapters so they flowed more beautifully than I could ever have done on my own.

So much gratitude to all the amazing friends and mentors I have met along the way. You know who you are, and there are too many to list. Thanks to my podcast guests for their wisdom and their vulnerability and the clients who helped me grow.

Your patience, kindness, and grace have taught me so much about myself and about being part of a community.

To my amazing colleagues at Invis Pacific View Mortgages and Vanisle Veterinary Hospital. You inspire me daily, and I value each of you for your friendship and teamwork. To my writing meditation group, thank you for re-awaking my love of pen and paper and for an hour of peace and joy that I look forward to every day.

Lastly, thank you to my Toastmasters family. Each chapter is really just a speech transcribed into words. Much gratitude for always being a safe place to bounce off ideas

Overcoming Awkward:
The Introvert's Guide to Networking, Marketing, & Sales

By Monica Parkin

TABLE OF CONTENTS

CHAPTER 1 – STARTING OUT

*"Be Yourself. Everybody else is
already taken."*
~ Oscar Wilde

Have you ever wondered what you would say to your younger self if you could travel back in time and talk to them? I do. There are so many things I would say to my younger self to prepare her for the future and give her all the advantages I now know that she would need. The problem is that I don't know if I would even recognize her to introduce myself. The person I am today is so completely different that I don't think I would know the old me even if I ran straight into her. And would the earlier version of me listen to the older, wiser, and more experienced version of me? Would she appreciate the heads up about all of the things that are to come? Or would she smirk and walk away, choosing to do whatever she wanted anyhow?

It's a great philosophical question. But it is also an important one because, just as there is a past *you*, there is a future *you*. And the future *you* is trying to share vast stores of knowledge with *present* you. How can you access that knowledge today to maximize your opportunities and build the life you are destined to live? The best way to access future knowledge is to borrow from the knowledge that is available all around you.

Today, most people know me as a successful entrepreneur. I own several thriving businesses, I'm a keynote speaker, a speaking coach, and a podcast host. I am active in several industries and in my community, I have more friends than I can count, and I genuinely enjoy getting to know people.

What most people don't know is that I was not always this person. In fact, I was not even remotely close.

Growing up, I was the "odd kid" at school. I was introverted, socially awkward, and I struggled with ADHD. Back then if you were different, you had to learn to live with it or be crushed by a system that was not designed to cater to anyone outside the traditional norms.

When I struggled with focusing in class, I was told that I just had to "try harder" to sit still and "stop interrupting." When I struggled socially or found it difficult to not interrupt the teacher, I was banished from the classroom. I spent most of my time either standing out in the hallway for being disruptive in class or sitting alone reading a book because I didn't know how to make friends. Gym class was filled with potential issues like the choosing of teams for sports because I was always one of the last ones picked or, if I <u>was</u> picking, I wasn't brave enough to speak up and choose in case I made the wrong choice.

My school years represented a pretty isolating time during which I spent most of my days with imaginary friends I found on the pages of books. When I tore myself away from the wonderful escape books provided, I was forced back into the "real world" where I had to wonder what was wrong with me and why I couldn't just make friends or join a conversation with ease like other people did.

I tried several tactics to address my anemic social circle. I would get new hairstyles or ask my mom to take me shopping for new clothes, thinking that if I could just look a certain way and fit in that I could pass as "normal," but the differences between myself and everyone else always stuck out no matter how I changed my outward appearance. That's because those differences were far more than skin deep.

I felt socially isolated and my primary friendships were with adults or imaginary friends. I had no idea that someday I would experience a level of success and joy and abundance and connection beyond my wildest dreams. Not only that but the things about me that made me different would one day become my most valuable commodities.

So how did the transformation take place? How did a shy, socially awkward introvert like me turn into a master relationship builder? And are the lessons I learned available to everyone else? Even you? Well, the answer is that you can evolve. You can do it without trying to be someone you are not. That's right. You can be authentically you while maximizing all of the unique qualities you alone possess. I am going to share with you exactly how.

First, let me give a bit more history and context.

Notes

CHAPTER 2 – HOW IT ALL BEGAN

"Carve your name on hearts, not tombstones. A legacy is etched into the minds of others and the stories they share."
~Shannon Alder

In 2016, my husband and I bought a new house. Some people have horror home purchase stories. Not us! We had a great experience with the mortgage broker who helped us get approved. It was such a positive experience, in fact, that I decided I'd like to try it out as a career. I paid for the course, studied hard and, eleven months later, passed the exam. Shortly thereafter, I started interviewing brokerages to see which one might be a good fit. What an exciting time it was in my life. But I did not have a complete picture of what it would be. I thought my days would consist of inputting numbers and giving people the good news that they had been approved for the homes of their dreams. Wow, was I ever wrong.

What I quickly found out is that 50% of the work of a mortgage broker is solving complex problems and coming up with creative solutions, and the other 50% is sales and building relationships. I had this idea that I could just work from home or sit behind a desk all day expecting that business would just come to me. I was a total introvert with massive social anxiety. When I found out I would need to go out, be among the people, "network," go to events, and promote myself, I just about quit on the spot.

In fact, my first reaction was, "I did not sign up for this!!!"

Only the fact that I had just spent the previous year studying, submitting assignments, studying for a grueling exam, and spending money to activate my license stopped me from throwing in the towel right then and there.

I could not allow my investment to be wasted. Besides, I was not one to shrink from a challenge; and this was a big one!

To make matters even worse, I was not even able to sit with the idea for a while and get adjusted to the idea. The first week, there was a Chamber of Commerce Networking dinner, and it was suggested that I go with my office colleagues and use it as a chance to make myself known to the local business community. Everything in me was screaming "NO!" but peer pressure is a powerful thing. My colleagues encouraged me to go along. I agreed, thinking that since I would be there with them, it might not be so bad.

Wrong.

It was far worse than I had imagined. I got there early and walked inside, could not find a single face in the crowd I knew, and promptly went back out to my car where I sat having an anxiety attack. I spent the next several minutes trying to talk myself out of going back home. In the end, just as I was planning my escape and excuse for not going, one of my colleagues drove up and I had no choice but to walk in with them.

I reluctantly made my way inside and looked for someone I knew. But, to my chagrin, the room was full of strangers and they were all mingling around and talking to each other like old friends. I felt like a lost toddler in a crowd of strangers. I couldn't get up the nerve to walk up to a group of people and join the conversation.

Again, I wanted to leave, but my colleagues already knew I was here and it was too late to make a quiet exit. I would have to bite the proverbial bullet.

Instead, I did what had worked for me in other socially awkward contexts like high school dances: escape and hide. I retreated to the bathroom and spent most of my time "fixing my makeup" and scrolling through my phone until dinner was announced.

At that point, I made my way over to sit at a table with my colleagues. There was an available seat, so I breathed a sigh of relief, relaxed a bit, and sat, knowing I would be comfortable making conversation with people I knew.

Throughout the night, though, I had to keep talking myself out of leaving. That voice in my head from many years of social anxiety kept saying "I can't do this. It's too hard. It's not me." The loudest voice in my head offered me a solution: "Just go home!"

I had no idea how to talk to people, what to say, where to put my hands, or even how to stand. It felt awkward and weird to be face-to-face with others having to share my thoughts and exchange ideas with them. So many obstacles confronted me as a social awkward introvert.

Do I smile or do I not smile? If I do smile, how long a smile is too long. Is my smile coming off as a creepy smile or friendly smile? Do I put my hands in my pockets? Or is that too casual? On my hips? Or is that too stern?

By my side? No, that's too awkward. Is this too much eye contact? Have I been looking away too long? OMG!!! Why is there no class out there for where to put your hands and how long to make eye contact with people?

I was making myself crazy with all the social cues I did not understand and wondered why this comes so naturally to some people but was so impossibly hard for me? Am I broken? What is my problem, I am 42 years old, for goodness' sake, I should know how to do this by now!

I finally figured out that the best place for my hands was holding a drink, but I'm not really a drinker. So, I would just buy ginger ale or soda water to try to keep my hands busy. But then I would forget what the drink was there for and look down to see that I had gulped it all down in my nervousness. Or I would hover by the appetizer table and pretend to be examining all the food, but you can only do that for so long before you start to look weird.

I got through the evening but not without feeling awkward, out of place, and a little bit traumatized by the overwhelming social interaction. I had no idea you could actually feel lonely in a room full of people, but I did that night. I looked around and couldn't find another person who looked as out of place as me.

The idea of shaking hands and handing out cards was terrifying but I did it. I handed out cards, I sold myself, I told people how I could offer the best rates and get them the best mortgage and I came home with a pocket full of business cards.

When I got home, I pulled out all the cards I had collected that night and realized that I would never call any of them. I had not connection with any of them, I had just listened to their pitch with no intention of ever calling them. I decided to throw the cards in the fire. As I did so, the realization hit me that if I was throwing away their cards, that meant they were likely throwing away my cards too! That meant I had just put myself through a horrible experience for no reason!

That night I vowed that I needed to do something about it. One thing was clear: no one could fix this problem but me.

If I wanted to succeed in this industry where success relied heavily on a person's ability to network and build relationships, I was going to have to get past my social anxiety. Thankfully, I was also enough of a reader and an intellectual to know that I needed to retrain my brain. The source of the problem was deeply embedded inside me. I would have to get down to the root and pull it out!

Notes

CHAPTER 3 - THE BRAIN'S SUPERHIGHWAYS

"Biology gives you a brain. Life turns it into a mind."
~ Jefferey Engenides

My life was not without victories I could draw knowledge from. I thought about all the things I had overcome in the past and how I had done those things. A good example was when I was in labour with my first child. Every time I would change position, the pain of my contractions would worsen, and I would want to be back to the previous position. The Doula I had hired to guide me through labor would remind me each time that "it's only harder for the first few contractions and then your body will adapt to the new position, and it will be easier. It feels harder now but your labour will progress faster and you will have an easier birth if you push through these position changes and let your body adjust to them so it can do its work."

There was a great lesson to be learned there and one many of us miss. Whenever we attempt to make a change in our lives, we feel the pain of change that comes from losing what we had even if it was harming us in some way. We found our old way to be familiar and comfortable. We might have been in pain, but it was a pain we knew. Change requires facing newness. New positions. New people. New places. New challenges. Familiarity is replaced by novelty and we have to adapt. Sometimes, temporarily, that is just as painful as staying the same.

Then I thought about smaller, more inconsequential things like developing a palate for coffee. At first, I hated it. It smelled nothing like it tasted. The aroma was warm and inviting. But the taste was bitter even when masked by cream and sugar. But I persisted.
After a while, my taste buds conformed. Coffee started to taste good and then, eventually, I started to actually crave it. I decided if it was possible to learn to love something as disgusting as coffee was the first time I tried it, maybe it was possible with behaviours too.

Why would anyone learn to like coffee or respond to advice about labor positions? It can only be because of the benefits that await us on the other side of change. As we grow, in even the smallest ways, the change is hard but the payoff is often worth it.

The brain works with a complex construct of super sensory capabilities. The brain can process millions of pieces of information to reach a single conclusion. This is done with the help of neural pathways in the brain that you have been building (and destroying) your entire life. It's how we learn language. When babies are born, they are able to understand hundreds of different sounds. But the brain is remarkable in its ability to preserve only those neural pathways that correspond to the spoken language of the child's family. If the family speaks two languages, the child's brain will save the pathways it needs for both. All others decay.

But as remarkable as the brain's ability to discard neural pathways is its ability to create brand new ones. That's right. Your brain is an ongoing construction site. When your brain thinks about any particular thing again and again, the neural pathways involved in that thought process get wider and wider.

And if the brain is presented with brand new information for which it has no neural pathways, it will simply create them! And we are just at a primitive level of understanding how incredibly plastic the brain is and all that it can do.

Neurologists have come up with a little slogan: "cells that fire together, wire together." This indicates that your cells are intelligent in their ability to accommodate whatever load you give them to carry. Connecting one neuron with another in the brain creates a tiny pathway. But those two neurons continue to connect with others until it creates a wide path that is smooth and highly functional.

Somehow, my brain got wired to be fearful and awkward in my own skin. It doesn't matter why it happened or how it happened.

That is an exercise for a different kind of expert. My job was to undo those negative neural pathways and teach my brain to build new ones. I mean, really, what did I have to lose? If I walked away from where I was, I would be throwing away 12 months of school, a lot of money, and a lot of lost opportunities. I could even, potentially, be throwing away friendships and business relationships I would treasure for a lifetime.

I made myself a deal: I would try it for a month. If it worked and I saw a change, great; if not, I would quit my job. No regrets. Giving myself an out at the end allowed my brain to relax. This would not be forever; it was just for today. Tomorrow, I would reassess.

I started with a bold decision to reframe my thoughts and say a mantra to myself that was the polar opposite of what I had always said in the past. My new mantra would be: "I like people, I like getting to know people, and building relationships is fun." This is what I would focus on for the next 30 days without worrying about the outcome. It was a great strategy because it gave me a challenge with an end date. If it turned out to be sheer torture, I could comfort myself with the knowledge that it would be over in a month.

This works for everything by the way. Facing challenges in small manageable chunks is the cornerstone of most successful mindset changes. People often try to make sweeping changes in their lives and declare grand promises for the future. The brain sees this as new information but it doesn't have a sufficient neural highway on which to process your claim. So, the excitement, resolve, and commitment you feel at the start quickly fizzle out. It's no wonder. You ran out of road, so the idea had nowhere to go.

Addiction recovery programs use the slogan "just for today" for a reason. If an addict focuses too far ahead and thinks about having to give up their substance of choice for a lifetime, it's too much for the brain to process. They cave and talk themselves out of it. But if it's "just for today" or one day at a time, they can stay sober and start to implement new habits. The brain has time to destroy the old pathways that led to excess. They form a new outlook that starts to be more desirable than the old one.

The first day I put this into practice I found myself in the lineup at the grocery store and the clerk tried to make conversation. You know, when they pick up your bank card and read your name and then start calling you by your name as if they know you. "Hey, Monica, how is your day going, did you find everything you needed today? Oh, dog food! What kind of dog do you have?"

To be honest that would normally really piss me off. I would be thinking, "Don't talk to me like you know me. We're not friends. I don't want to chat with you. And why are announcing my name to the entire store? Also, my dogs are none of your business." But today was the first day of my plan to try to build new habits. So, instead of putting my head down as if I didn't hear her, offering a barely audible response, or pretending to be looking for imaginary lost items in my purse, I said to myself, "Remember you like people now. You like getting to know people. Why don't you try answering her just for practice? If you hate it, you never have to do it again."

Notice, I again gave myself an out, and I focused on the current situation — not every future situation. I said, "just this once" and "if you don't like it, you never have to do it again." That kept me focused on the current moment and made it less overwhelming and more manageable.

I responded with a smile and told her what kind of dog I had, and the world didn't fall apart. I smiled and she smiled back. She told me that one of my items was 2 for 1 and, if I wanted to grab another, there would be no charge. I was like "Holy cow! Really?" It was an expensive item, and I would never have found that out if I was pretending not to hear her. So far, this experiment was working out in my favor.

You can use this technique with anything. Almost a year ago I stopped eating sugar and I still take it day by day moment by moment. I never say to myself, "you are never eating sugar again." I say, not this time, "just for this meal don't pick up sugar. If you want it later, you can have it then." Later, when faced with that temptation, I take it a moment at a time all over again.

Throughout the first day, I made an effort, if not to talk to people, at least to be open to responding to them. As a result, the most amazing things started to happen. I started to feel connected. I got interesting news and tidbits about events. At the end of the day, I went home and reviewed all the good things that had happened as a result of being willing to talk to people. I was building my "people-person highway."

Every day it got a little easier and I became a little more willing to take another tiny step in the right direction. Two weeks into this experiment, I was at my mailbox and my neighbor drove up. I hated talking to neighbors.

My theory was that nothing good came from getting to know neighbors. It meant having to go to their BBQs and to listen to their complaints or be asked to feed their cat when they went on vacation. The old me would have jumped in my car and driven off right away, but the ncw me had a moment of hesitation about that escape plan.

After two weeks of positive interactions, I told myself "What's the worst that would happen if you just stayed and said hello?" And that's what I did. My neighbor lived down the street from me for three years, but we had never met. She walked up, introduced herself, and seemed delighted to finally meet me. She was actually a really nice person and she told me that in the mornings when she left for work, there was often a mother bear and cubs sleeping in the ditch right outside my gate. I was amazed that I never knew this having lived there for three years.

That night when I was celebrating the wins, I said, "Wow, if I had not talked to her, I would not know to look for bears when I leave in the morning. How amazing is that?"

Just like the coffee I hated the first time but grew to crave, these little tastes of community and interaction made me start to want more. I found myself starting ever so slowly to initiate conversations. I became that person in the grocery line that I formerly hated because I would say hello and start talking to people. When clients came in, instead of just talking about their finances and then shooing them out the door, I asked them about themselves, their families, their interests. I found out the most amazing things about other people and started to look forward to the conversations that came in between the finance-related questions.

I still was not ready to go to a big, crowded event, but I knew I needed to make some strides in that direction. So, I found some online groups in my industry, and I made an effort to contribute. I answered questions when people asked them, I shared my experiences, and I even posted the occasional meme or industry-related joke. I started to connect in new ways.

Notes

CHAPTER 4 – YOU'RE AN ORIGINAL. ACT LIKE ONE

"The privilege of a lifetime is to become who you truly are."
— *Carl Gustav Jung*

A few months in I was making some progress on overcoming my social anxiety but I was still really struggling to actually get clients and find my niche. I reached out to others who knew more. I thought, "I'm going to reach out to some of the people in this industry that are really successful. I'm going to learn all I can from them."

I was a member of a Facebook group called "Women in the Mortgage Industry," and there were people there who were super willing to help out newcomers and answer questions. Many of them had offered to help when I first started, they would say, "You can call me any time. You can ask me questions. I see that you're new. I'm here to help."

I took a chance and called some of them up to ask what they were doing and how they built their businesses. I wasn't getting any real leads. I was doing these Facebook ads that were not working and posting all kinds of business content but none of it was getting me any traction and I was getting really frustrated. I decided to call some of those wonderful and successful women who offered to help me. The problem was, once I got them on the phone, they all gave me the same answer:

"Just be your authentic self."

Easy for them to say! I was still discovering my authentic self. My background had been so rocky from a social perspective, I had little confidence in my authentic self. I didn't like the first answer so I called another woman. She also said, "Just be yourself. Be you! There's no magic strategy. Don't buy leads. Don't go around handing out business cards, don't spend money on flyers. Just be yourself."

I didn't like that advice either (I'm a slow learner sometimes), so I called yet another one. She said the same thing and I started to get annoyed. I mean how could I be myself when I was awkward, shy, and uncomfortable?

"Be yourself?" I scowled into the phone as I hung up.

That's what we tell kids in elementary school where they don't know how to make friends. Someone has told me that my whole life: "Just be yourself." I thought, "This is crap, they don't want to help me, they just want to keep all the business to themselves!" But I sat with it for a few days and since nothing else was working I eventually thought "what do I really have to lose?"

I spent some time thinking about what it meant to be my authentic self. I realized that it's not just a phrase or a philosophy. It's an action. I needed to "be me."

Being yourself means showcasing who you are and what you are interested in. There were a few things I did know about myself. For one thing... I was the crazy goat lady! I love goats and chickens and pretty much anything with fur or feathers. It was a great place to start. It had nothing to do with finance but people don't want to hear about your business all the time, they want to get to know you. Real Authentic you.

I started to put my real self out there and show people that quirky part of me. Guess what? It worked! Turns out people really connect to quirky crazy goat lady! I started to post less business and more authentic me. I posted pics of myself out in the barn working with the animals.

I showed myself at the ice rinks in my crazy hats picking my kids up from hockey and screwing up recipe ideas and failing and having fun doing it. It was all raw and real. No filters. No airbrushing. No fancy glossy photos. I literally showed myself ankle-deep in goat poop wearing my old gum boots. It was just me being myself. And funnily enough, magical things started to happen. People started to connect to me, to who I am, and they loved seeing my life in a rural community.

Slowly but surely, my phone started to ring as a result of the other parts of my life I shared with the world. I started to get leads from people in my little community.

People would say, "Hey, I've got a rural property. I see you're a mortgage broker. Can you help me out with that?" In my head I was thinking, "No. I don't know the first thing about financing rural properties," but instead I said, "Absolutely! Let me find out about that and get back to you." Then I went and called my colleagues so they could guide me. I asked them, "What can I do? What lenders do I go to?" I got that file done. And from that came another file. From that file came another file and you see where this is going right?

I continued posting about the real quirky me and it turns out that me, the me I had never shown the world before, was someone people could connect to — someone they could relate to and trust.

One week I had been out all day looking for my dog that had gotten out. And I had stopped somewhere to ask if anyone had seen him and two weeks later, a lady came into my office because she saw me out looking for my dog. Guess what? She needed a mortgage.

I asked how she found me. She said that she saw me out looking for my dog and she recognized me from social media as being a mortgage broker. She loved dogs and wanted to work with someone who also loves dogs. She believed that dog people are good people. (That's true, you know.) She said she had made up her mind and that I had to be her mortgage broker.

And out of being me — out of being my quirky, little, weird self, came another client.

So, the lesson of this entire chapter is really just to be you. There really is no one better you can be. Everything else is fake and people see that. If you love to dance or you love to be out in nature or you are addicted to needlepoint — whatever it is — showcase that.

People don't want to hear about your business all the time. They want to hear about you!

We live in a "Pick me!" culture. Everyone seems to want attention. Selfies are proof of that. People want to be seen. This mindset has spilled over into marketing and advertising where people keep pushing the envelope to get the world's attention. Consumers are inundated with "pick me for this reason," "pick me for that reason." It's never-ending. If you really want to set yourself apart from the competition, show people who you really are — your authentic self.

There are always a thousand reasons to count yourself out:

- Too old,
- Too young.
- Too fat.
- Too thin.
- Too ugly.
- Too beautiful (seriously?).
- Too experienced.
- Too inexperienced.
- Too unique
- Not unique enough
- Too shy
- Too outgoing

None of those reasons are valid. When people choose a service, they don't choose that service because of a flashy ad. They choose that service because they liked the person behind it. Because you made a connection with them.

Notes

CHAPTER 5 – DEMOLISHING THE COMFORT ZONE

*"When you're socially awkward,
you're isolated more than usual,
and when you're isolated more than
usual, your creativity is less
compromised by what has been said
and done. All your hope in life
starts to depend on your craft, so
you try to perfect it... Being the off
one out may have its temporary
disadvantages, but more
importantly, it has its permanent
advantages.
~ Criss Jami*

Have you ever noticed something a little bit strange about Bill Gates, Elon Musk, Meryl Streep, J. K. Rowling, and Warren Buffet? Like noticing that they are brilliant at what they do but seem to have a hard time talking about it? Have you seen them talking with their heads down or averting their eyes away? Have you noticed their affect is a bit strange as if they can't wait until their interviews are over when they have to talk about themselves?

But get them talking about the thing they love — computers, spaceships, acting, writing, and finance, and something turns on inside them like a motor revving up for 200 laps at NASCAR!? That "thing" you see is the classic introvert syndrome.

Some of the most famous people in the world are introverts. An article by Lindsay Pietroluongo in the blog, *Elegant Themes,* describes this phenomenon masterfully:

> *Introverts are often (and mistakenly) thought to be any or all of the following: Aloof, awkward, loners, nerdy, unfriendly, shy, strange, or withdrawn.*

That certainly describes me and, perhaps you if you picked up this book among the many choices you had. You have always felt more comfortable alone or in your small, safe, circle of friends. You were misunderstood — perhaps outcast. But there was something about you that sparks and lights up the sky. For me, that was animals.

It is a fact that I nearly missed when I decided to start advertising. I felt like I had nothing to offer people. Nobody is attracted to a post with words like "adjustable rate," "amortization," or "penalty calculation." What else did I have to offer? Me? No way! Being me was not enough. Or was it? Would it be possible to put myself out there and connect with people about something that lit me up inside?

Lucky for me, a new networking group started up in our town that had a unique format. Instead of people standing around mingling, one person would pitch their idea and the rest of the group would take turns giving feedback. It was a way to speak and get to know people in an organized fashion with clear guidelines rather than have people stand around, meet randomly, and make small talk. As I showed up week after week and started to get to know other business owners, I looked forward to meet ups and even pitched my own business.

At one of the meetings, my friend Amy Englemark mentioned that she went to a group called Toastmasters and that it was a great place to learn to speak in a fun and supportive atmosphere. I sought them out and showed up at a meeting. Honestly, I very nearly turned around and walked right back out. But someone came up and introduced themselves, offered me a pamphlet, and said that I should sit down as the meeting was starting right away.

I watched in admiration and interest as people gave speeches and then got feedback that was positive and encouraging. I was intrigued when the meeting moved onto something called table topics. Everyone took turns speaking on the spot for two minutes about random topics. I was terrified to try one but, after a few meetings, I found I quite liked the challenge of speaking on my feet.

People said I was good at conveying my ideas and that they were looking forward to my first speech. I felt part of a community, and my confidence grew. As I got better at organized speeches in front of a group, I naturally got better at small talk and mingling too. I started to look forward to group events so I could talk to people and find out more about them. I learned to ask open-ended questions, and I learned that people love to talk about themselves. Surprisingly, I discovered that I love to hear their stories.

My newfound confidence and ability to connect spread to other areas of my life. I could hardly believe it when I heard myself volunteer to be a hockey team manager for my son's team. I was equally surprised to find I enjoyed it. It was a great chance to get to know other parents. I was on a roll. I then stepped up to serve on my kids' school PAC and, in working closely with other parents on projects, I got to know them on a deeper level. Relationships and friendships began to form with other parents and administrators.

Remember the old me who used to arrive late for functions or sit in my car so I would not be standing around with no one to talk to? Well, the new me started to arrive early. I did this partly because I wanted to put those people at ease who used to be just like me. I made a point of seeking out new people and asking about themselves to make them feel welcome. I learned that some of the best conversations happened before events even got going. I started to look forward to going to events where I didn't know anyone because I saw it as an opportunity to meet new people, build new relationships, and to discover new things.

Somehow, over the course of a few years, I went from sitting in my car or the bathroom afraid of talking to strangers, not knowing what to say or how to stand, to being an award-winning public speaker, hosting a podcast, and working as a director of Community Engagement where my sole job is getting to know people in my community. I did this by "acting as if."

"Acting as if" is a powerful mantra I learned as I was developing the new me. It simply means that you don't have to become something to act as if you have already.

You can propel yourself to the future where you are already living and thriving by simply acting as if you are already there. I pretended I was someone I wasn't until I became that person.

At my core, am I still an introvert? Yes. Do I enjoy a quiet evening at home in my PJs with a good book? Yes. I am wired the way I am wired. There is nothing wrong with being more comfortable in one environment than another. The problem was that, when I stepped out of that comfort zone, I froze like a deer in headlights. I didn't have a mechanism to support me when I changed from my PJs to my power suit and walked out of my house into the big, wide world.

Today, I love the opportunity to go to events, meet people, hear people's stories, and build relationships. I can have the best of both worlds now and so can you.

In the next chapter, I am going to give you some concrete ideas and suggestions about how to do just that: meet people and build relationships. Never fear! We will do this slowly and gently. Not by throwing yourself into a party where you don't know anyone like I did, but by being your authentic self, and sharing your unique strengths and skill sets in small but tangible and noticeable ways.

Notes

CHAPTER 6 - MAKING CONNECTIONS WITH BABY STEPS

*"Everything you want in life is a
relationship away."*
~ Idowu Koyenikan

When you hear the term networking, what does it bring to mind?

When I went to business school, it meant something completely different than what it does now. I remember taking a class about networking and marketing where we learned about networking and we had to practice it. Essentially, we learned that it was walking around at a party, handing out business cards, shaking people's hands saying, "Hi, my name is _____, and my business is _____."

Then, we were supposed to go straight into our elevator pitch and start talking about ourselves and what was so great about our business or product. As an introvert, this used to absolutely terrify me. The idea of walking up to random strangers and talking about myself and selling them on a product was horrifying. And it *should* be terrifying and horrifying because it does absolutely nothing good for you or your business. No one enjoys it, and it alienates people rather than attracts them. Did it ever get results? Yes. But that was more because of persistence than persuasion.

This is not the way to build your business, and this strategy does not build relationships. Let's look for a moment at what the actual dictionary definition of networking is. It is "the exchange of information or services among individuals, groups, or institutions, specifically *the cultivation of productive relationships for employment or business.*"

Let's read that last line again: *"The cultivation of productive relationships."* The key word there is "relationships." Networking is not walking around shaking people's hands while passing out business cards. You might as well throw all those cards at the wall because, I don't know about you, but when I come home from an event like that, you know what I do with all those cards stuffed in my pocket? I throw them in the woodstove!

I literally never look at them again and, if I do, it is to add them to <u>my</u> mailing list so I can send them my newsletter. It's not because I am going to save their cards on the chance I might need their services in the future. If someone is interesting enough that I want to talk to them again, I google them or find them on social media. I do not dig their business card out of my wallet. It's frankly impossible to save all those business cards anyway.

I laugh now to think about how much I agonized over that first set of business cards. I spent hours staring at graphics, fonts, layouts, and examples of different cards. I spent a lot of time on the design, as if the actual eye appeal of my card would make any difference at all. When was the last time someone handed you a card and you made a purchasing decision based on how the card looked? Never! No one has ever said, "Wow, this plumber has mad graphic design skills, he is the guy I need to change out my hot water tank!" It's ridiculous, right?

In fact, I have zero desire to go buy a product or service from someone I met for two seconds who shook my hand and handed me a card. There's no connection there. None. If that's networking, I don't want to do it. I want to build connections, build relationships, create a beautiful web of people who are connected to each other and support and care about each other.

Now I'm not saying that having a good-looking business card doesn't matter, because it does. It still reflects on your attention to detail, particularly if you are in the design business. What I am saying is that it's not going to make or break your success on its own.

It's like an intricate spider web. I have my place in one spot on the web and I meet someone from another place on the web. They connect me with someone else somewhere else on the web or I help them make a connection to someone I am connected with on the web. They, in turn, use that connection to connect with someone else and all these people in all areas become part of my community.

Through this mindset, you can build webs of community, across different organizations, professions, and groups that all help each other. Your connections can span generations, industries, countries, etc. There is no limit.

How and where I connect with people has evolved since that first Chamber dinner and surprisingly, the 2020 COVID pandemic accelerated that process. Now I get to connect to people in other ways with more creativity and on different platforms.

When I do go to a physical event, I don't go to hand out my cards or talk about myself or pitch my business. I go with the intent of listening more than talking, asking questions, and really engaging. Connection and relationships are built when you *listen* — not when you talk. I recently talked with Susan Thomas, VP of Eastern Canada for Invis and Mortgage Intelligence, and she said that she used the "ear-to-mouth ratio." She said we have two ears and one mouth, so we should spend two-thirds of our time listening and one-third of our time talking. I loved that analogy and have found it to be exactly true.

I ask a lot of questions and not just because I think people like to talk about themselves. I am genuinely interested in getting to know them and how I might connect them to someone else they can be of service to. I never stand there anymore wondering what to say or if I should smile or where to put my hands. I am genuinely happy to be there, happy to meet them, and interested in what they have to say and it shows in my posture.

When I meet people, my face is naturally warm and open because I am genuinely curious. People cannot articulate what it is about me that they like because our connection is visceral. My body is naturally relaxed and comfortable because I am doing something that brings me joy and that is connecting with other humans.

My openness combined with my relaxation puts them at ease. I never wonder what to say anymore. I just ask questions "What is your business? Interesting, what made you decide to go into this line of work? Who is your ideal customer? What do you love about what you do? What is your biggest challenge?" Then I listen to their stories, I soak in their passion, and I look for opportunities to be of service. Who can I connect them to? How can I help them grow?

One of the last meetings I went to before the COVID pandemic was a brand-new group for me where I knew very few people. The old me would have been freaked out, but the new me was excited at the opportunity to hear so many people's stories and to build new connections. I didn't see a room full of strangers; I saw a room full of future friends and colleagues.

The first person I talked to was in the middle of starting a blog/website that showcased different restaurants and food. She would post about menus and events with photos of dishes and reviews. It was sort of a "where to go eat tonight" kind of website.

I said I thought it sounded amazing and that my husband and I went for date night once a week and would totally use that service. Then I asked her what inspired it. It turns out that she and her husband also like to go out but can never decide where to go. Her eyes lit up at the chance to talk about the thing she created and loved. She became engaged and excited as I dug deeper and asked more questions out of genuine interest.

She said she was passionate about local organic food and had some food sensitivities, so she had to be careful about where she ate and what was on the menu. In the process of doing research for herself she discovered this was an issue for other people too, so she wanted to share that information with them. Immediately, I liked her and loved her idea because she had identified a need in her own life and turned it into an opportunity to serve others and also to create a business that was thriving.

As I was speaking to her, I remembered that I had a friend in another group who does food and restaurant tours. She picks people up at the airport or hotel or home and shows them the sights.

She may take them to a local winery or a farm that makes the food and then onto a restaurant to eat food that came from that farm for a truly immersive experience.

I thought that since they were both passionate about local food and supporting high-quality producers, they should connect. I asked for her website address and said that I had someone I thought she should meet. When I got home, I looked up my other friend and I composed an email to both of them:

Hey Cheryl, meet Barb. You are both really passionate about high-quality local produce and the restaurants that serve it, you both have food sensitivities and cater to people who do. I think there is an opportunity here for both of you to collaborate. Cheryl writes a blog about where to go and what places cater to what sensitivities and serve food from what farms. Barb this will be a huge help to you in your business as all the research has already been done for you.

Cheryl, I know you want your website and blog to grow as you work to reach more people. If you had a section on your site about local tours for visitors and tourists, it would grow your reach and be of service to those in your market.

Boom! Connection made. Web extended. I just helped two other entrepreneurs and grew my own personal network in the process.

Reciprocity is a beautiful thing, and this is how it starts. Now if I had written, "Hey, Cheryl, I can get you listed on this blog, but I want you to pay me a percentage of the revenue that comes from it," it would not have been effective. My email might have been ignored or worse, deleted. If I had written, "I am going to connect you with someone who can help you grow your business and I hope you will return the favour by sending me a referral sometime," I would have ruined the offer.

Let's take that a step further.
If I had even thought that either business owner owed me something for this favour — even if I did not state that outright — it would have changed the intent of my email and both women would have sensed it. They would have viewed my email with a sense of obligation. I didn't want any of those things. I just saw two people who could help each other out and wanted to connect them both.

When you do things just to be kind and help your fellow entrepreneurs grow, beautiful things flow from that. I think you know where this is going, right?

I didn't ask for it, I didn't even think about it at the time, but good things did come from that organically. The results did not happen that month. It often does not happen right away. It could take a year or more. But it almost always happens that reciprocity works its magic and brings that goodwill back to you.

A year later, when Barb was picking up a tourist to go on a tour and they mentioned they were here house hunting, who do you think Barb told them to call about a mortgage? You guessed it! Me! Why? Not because I had ever once talked about my mortgage business or told her what an awesome broker I am, but because I showed her (vs. told her) what kind of person I am and proved that I was invested in her success. That is how we build authentic real connections with others.

Most of my best connections and most valuable relationships have come from helping others to grow. When you help others, you help yourself. It's all about being part of a community. When your community grows, you grow too.

Think of it like buying a house in a neighborhood and fixing that house up. You work hard to turn that house into the most beautiful space. Perhaps you have had the house designed and remodeled by the most famous architect in the world. You choose every fabric with care and use only the best material. It has a gorgeous yard with breathtaking landscaping and a driveway full of luxury cars.

Now imagine that next door, there is a house that is abandoned with boards nailed to the windows. Across the street is a house that is falling down. There is a broken refrigerator and an old car sitting on the lawn. To your left is a house with weeds growing so high, you couldn't walk through them.

The windows are broken out and the house is in desperate need of a paint job. Guess what? All of the work you have done to make your home attractive and add to its property value is lost by the neighborhood. If your beautiful home is in the middle of a run-down neglected neighborhood, it loses all its value.

If your neighbors are suffering and economically depressed, there will be crime. If their yards are not kept up and their houses maintained, your property value goes down too. If they fight amongst themselves and try to outdo each other, it will be a miserable place to live. Your business is just one house in the neighborhood and that neighborhood consists of your fellow entrepreneurs. As you help other businesses around you to be profitable and thrive, it helps yours as well. A rising tide lifts all ships.

Expand it out further. Your community is your actual community. When you support minor hockey or your local women's shelter or the school book drive, you make life better not only for all your current and potential clients, but also for yourself.

Expand it again. Your industry is your country. As a citizen of Canada, when forest fires ravage another province, I step up to help because that's what we do. We do the same in the mortgage industry, we all try collectively to make it a better place. Do that in your industry. If you are in food service, support your fellow restaurateurs. If you are in the beauty industry, support other salon owners, collaborate, share what works and *grow your industry together.*

Just like your quality of life is determined somewhat by the economic and social health of your nation, your livelihood also depends on the health of your industry. That means getting involved in your industry and doing things that are best for your whole industry, not just for you.

In the mortgage industry, we have several huge Facebook forums where we all help each other. We answer questions for each other, advocate for positive changes in legislation and offer a form of mentoring to newbies. We are all from different and competing brokerages, but we come together to support one another in the common goal of supporting our businesses and our clients.

It also means that you must consider companion industries. The mortgage industry cannot thrive if the real estate industry is limping. The same is true of the construction industry. If new homes are not being built, new mortgages are not needed and people selling their homes in search of new construction might opt to stay put if the cost of lumber has tripled driving prices through the roof (pardon the pun).

If someone calls me and says they are working with another mortgage broker, but they are not happy with them, I don't say "great I can get this done for you," and start counting how much commission I am going to make by wooing that customer from another broker to myself.

Instead, I ask questions, I say, "What about the other broker is an issue?" Most times, it's something that is going to be an issue no matter where they go. Maybe they have bruised credit, and they cannot be approved for as much as they want, or they are being asked for a lot of documents that they don't want to dig up. Those are things that will happen no matter where they go. So, I take the time to educate them and redirect them back to their original broker. I only take over if it's clear they are being taken advantage of or are receiving truly horrible service. My fellow brokers are part of a bigger community and supporting them means we are all stronger as a result.

When you lift up your fellow entrepreneurs and industry colleagues and contribute to your community, you increase your own value. You are only as good as those you support and have relationships with. If I can help save the relationship between the broker and his or her client, who knows if that client will remember me when someone asks for a mortgage broker. They might mention my name.

I have a podcast called "Juggling without Balls," and on it I talk to successful women who have made great strides in life. I remember talking to Sue Finneron who owned a car dealership and was awarded the "citizen of the century" award in her community. What stood out most to me in the interview was when she said:

> *"My community gave me everything. Without them, I have no customers."*

That is the essence of networking. It is not about selling yourself; it is about being your authentic self and lifting others around you. When you do that, you build a community, and that community is what makes your business thrive. The selling part comes later, and we will talk about that more in future chapters.

The other thing we are doing when we help other entrepreneurs in our community is building a bigger reach. Other entrepreneurs are their own centers of influence; in other words, they influence the people whose lives they touch. You can reach more people by building a connection with someone who is a center of influence than by reaching out to all those individual connections one at a time.

Let me explain with a story. My ideal clients as a mortgage broker (and we'll talk about why it's important to know who that is later), are first-time home buyers and young people upgrading into a bigger home. To build trust and relationships with my target market, I would have to connect with a lot of people individually, and I would need to be where they are. I can do this to some degree with advertising and marketing, but it's not very personal. I can create blog posts and video blogs that are helpful to establish me as someone who is an expert, or I can place ads so I am more visible to them. I will reach some of them that way but it is a very random process. It's an improvement over handing out business cards to random strangers, but it is still less effective than getting to know these people personally.

Think back for a minute to a time when you got a job, or you hired someone. If you were a job-seeker, you may have applied for many positions.

If you were the employer, you may have sifted through a pile of resumes and maybe one stood out and you hired that candidate. Job seekers can investigate companies they apply to but, ultimately, they have to make their decision on limited information. That's a form of blind advertising. You make your decision based on the information presented because you don't have a personal connection.

If on the other hand you were looking for work and your friend said, "Hey, my company is hiring right now and you would love it here. I'll call him and put in a good word for you." That would change things for both of you. Not only does George feel more comfortable hiring you because your friend can vouch for you but you have a better chance at the job because George is a centre of influence, and one of the people he has influence over happens to know you.

Imagine you are looking for a lawyer when you are new in town and don't have anyone to ask. You may respond to an ad you saw on the side of a bus that you have seen a few times or you may go online and look at websites and choose the nicest one.

But what are you more likely to do when you are looking for a professional? What do you do? You ask someone you trust — your boss, your co-worker, your neighbor, maybe you post on social media, but rarely do you make those decisions without asking someone for a recommendation. Centers of influence are people who are likely to give recommendations and have those recommendations be taken seriously. They are often employers or professionals or people with large networks.

Last month my hot water tank broke down and, instead of going to google to look for a plumber, I asked my network. I posted on social media that I needed a plumber and asked people to make recommendations. Within minutes, I had ten answers and five of them were for the same person.

The recommendations came from centers of influence in my network. A notary I know from my business group said "Call Bill and tell him I sent you. He came out for me on Christmas day last year." A realtor I work with frequently also said, "Bill is your guy. He is reliable, and he does good work."

Here's the thing, both the notary and the realtor are centers of influence in their communities and on social media. They interact with a lot of other people who trust them every day and have relationships with other entrepreneurs and their clients. Bill built a relationship with them and now has instant social credibility as a result. When I asked who to use as a plumber on social media, not only did I see the answer, but all the people also that are on their social media saw it too.

I guarantee to you I was not the only one who benefited from that post. Other clients, friends, and family of both myself, and the people I asked saw that post and made a mental note to themselves that Bill is the guy to call. In fact, I know that is the case because in the next few weeks, no less than two people reached out to me to ask "Who was that plumber that was recommended to you? I saw the post and it looks like everyone recommended a certain guy. Was he good? Can you send me his info?"

Two things worked for Bill here. The first was having centers of influence to recommend him, and the second was to have social media amplify his credibility. Clearly, he had a great work ethic and gave consistently fair prices and good results. Otherwise, people would not have been comfortable recommending him.

So now we know that we need to build connections and community, in the next chapter I am going to show you where and how to do that.

Notes

CHAPTER 7 - IT TAKES A VILLAGE… AND SOCIAL MEDIA

"Social media is not a media. The key is to listen, engage, and build relationships."
~ David Alston

It doesn't just take a village to raise a child; it also takes a village to grow a business or fund a non-profit or amplify a cause. Think about what a village is; it is basically a set of people with different skill sets and different resources all working together for a common outcome.

61

But how do we grow our village in the first place? It's great to say" check-in with people and support their businesses and dreams." But what if you have spent your whole life in a bubble and you don't know anybody? How do you make those relationships in the first place, and how do you do it without walking around handing out business cards to strangers?

How do you turn strangers into friends and get to know them on a deeper level while, at the same time, highlighting your unique skill sets and contributing to your community? I am going to show you! And the best part is, you can do all those things and not spend a cent!

First, you need to figure out what you are passionate about and look to see where there is a need in your community. Then, volunteer! It doesn't matter where you volunteer, but it does matter that it is something you care deeply about. Offer your time freely, do a great job, and do it with no expectation of anything in return.

Volunteer Committees are an amazing way to showcase your skills, be of service to your community, and get to know people on a deeper level. When you sit with someone on a committee of any kind, you get a chance to meet as a group many times.

Over the course of those meetings, you really get to connect with people on a more personal level, build friendships, and have a chance to shine in your areas of strength.

I have a friend who is a web designer. Every year, she joins a new non-profit and offers her services to the organization. She updates their website, helps with press releases, and serves as the point of contact for anyone who needs something put on the organization's website. In doing this, she has not only had a chance to help out with organizations she is passionate about, but she's had literally hundreds of conversations with the people inside and outside of those organizations in her volunteer role. People get to see what she's like to work with and get to sample the kind of work she does. And she gets all of this exposure without even soliciting business from anyone. Many of those people come back to her or refer her when they are ready to have work done on their own websites.

Now I just want to caution you that this can backfire. This kind of commitment to an organization can work against you if it's not the right fit, if you are doing it for the wrong reasons, or if you do a poor job at the work product you provide. Volunteering and getting involved can amplify your strengths and build relationships. Done wrong or in excess, it can bring attention to your weaknesses and create divisions.

Wendy, for example, was a super busy mom who was excited to grow her business. Someone told her that volunteering was a great way to build her company.

She figured if a little volunteering was good, then a lot was great. Makes sense, right? Wrong! Wendy signed up to volunteer at six different organizations. She also had a business to work on and her own kids with extracurricular activities. With all those commitments, things started to slide and, before she knew it, she was in way over her head. She was not shining; she was drowning.

She was missing meetings and had so many different emails about so many different projects that she had signed up for, she was not able to read them all. People thought she was ignoring them. Or worse, people thought she was scatterbrained and disorganized.

She didn't have time to cultivate relationships or get to know people because she was always running to the next event.

Her business suffered and her personal life suffered because she was doing a half ass job at everything just trying to keep her head above water. She didn't show up prepared or engaged or ready to work. She was not someone anyone would send a referral too. Not only that, but she was not excited about a lot of the things she signed up for. They drained her energy and ate up her schedule. Her disdain showed in her attitude and her fellow committee members felt her lack of commitment. They resented her obvious disingenuousness towards something they were passionate about.

Don't be a Wendy. Get involved only if you have the time and interest to do a good job. Don't get involved just to put it on your list of volunteer activities. Choose a cause you are passionate about. Be sure you will work around people you want to work with doing a job that matches your skillset. If your skill set is accounting, volunteer for a financial role — if your abilities can support that. Be careful of stepping into a role you know nothing about or don't have time for. Better to do a good job at one thing than to do a poor job at five things.

Remember that on committees your personality traits are amplified because you are working in a group. If you are an amazing team player, that will be what people see. If you are a bit of a control freak and kind of a bossy pants, you are going to need to check those tendencies. Left unchecked, your fellow committee members will remember only the negatives about you.

When you are tempted to think that you have an amazing idea and it is the only way to go, that's the time to "shut the cluck up" and ask your fellow committee members what they think. True team players really hear and consider everyone's ideas. They are willing to consider other people's ideas without letting their own feelings get in the way. We don't build relationships by being right all the time; we do it by constantly asking, "How can I best serve this organization," and then getting out of our own way.

So now you have found some groups to be a part of. You have brought your skill sets into the group and are starting to get to know people. Now what?

Here's the thing about relationships, they rarely grow on their own. They take work and cultivation. And they're a two-way street. You must nurture them on a regular basis. You can't just form a relationship with someone and then not talk to them for a year only to reach out to them when you need something from them. If you want quality relationships to keep going and growing, you need to care for them.

We will talk more about this later but relationships are like crops; you can't just plant a seed and expect it to grow. They need food, water, sunlight, and attention. Once you start a relationship, you need to continue to nurture it.

Once you have done the work, gone out there and met people, you have completed the first step. Now you need to keep the relationship momentum going, *you need to nourish it.* Just like you need to follow up and communicate with clients, you need to follow up and check-in on relationships. But the check-in must be genuine. Human beings are uniquely skilled at spotting a fraud or a poser.

Remember I said when you meet someone that your job is to listen? If you did a good job listening, then you will have some details to start to build a relationship on.

You will have something of value to say when you follow-up that will be meaningful. This is your opportunity to follow up, to check-in, and to strengthen the connection you started when you got curious and asked them about themselves.

Let me illustrate this with a story. I met Lisa when we served together on a committee for a local charity. As part of our time together she divulged that she bought a fabulous outdoor pizza oven. I loved the idea of cooking pizzas outdoors with my kids so I got the details from her about the brand and where to buy it.

When I purchased it, I sent her a quick text with a photo that said, "Hey look what I got today. Thanks for the idea!"

That, in turn, became a conversation about what model number I got, how many people was I cooking for, and did I have any recipes yet. She sent me a link to the Facebook group about the oven, she gave me her favourite recipe, and she shared some pointers with me. All of these were fabulous. I used them all to create the best post COVID pizza party ever.

After I had used it the first time, I dropped her another note to update her and let her know how my party went, which recipe I had used, what was awesome, and what I needed to work on. See what was happening?

We went from just sitting on a committee together to having at least one common interest. But just one was enough to get started. We had something we could both mutually share and get excited about, and a relationship was starting to grow. It was a lot of fun to chat with her from time to time. It took very little effort on my part other than sharing my own excitement with her over my purchase and giving her an opportunity to share her knowledge and experience about the product with me.

I did not have to go knock on her door or pick up the phone and cold call her. It was organic and easy and natural. If you are a phone person you could do that, and it might work. It just happens that I am not a phone person. I actually kind of freeze up when I have to make a call. It feels very awkward and uncomfortable for me, but I'm totally happy to email someone or text someone.

You have to do what works for you because that is when you will be your most warm and authentic self. If you hate the phone and force yourself to make calls, it will come through on the call. If you hate texting and you try to check-in that way, that will come through also.

That's not to say there is not a time and a place for all forms of communication. There are times when I must pick up the phone and call someone. Anytime a topic is complicated or emotional, it demands a phone call. That is just how it is.

You cannot and should not solve big issues by text or email; it lacks the extra layers that you need for deep problem solving and unwinding complexities. What I'm talking about right now though is just checking in and staying in touch. You can do it in whatever way you feel more comfortable with because you will be your best self if you feel at ease.

What communication method are you most comfortable using? How do you feel when you pick up the phone, when you get a text, when you have to send an email? If it feels natural and easy, that's probably your default communication method. If you get a knot in your stomach, you find yourself overthinking, or you get anxious about it, then that's probably not your natural communication style.

It's like muscles; if you don't work them, they will atrophy. The same goes for your relationships and your communication skills. We've all got that friend — that one person who you only hear from when they want something from you. How do you feel when they call? You see their number and you think "What do they want this time?" Don't be that person! Be the person who is curious, who wants to learn about other people, and who wants to hear other people's stories.

When you meet someone, one of the first things you should be doing is taking a minute to invite them to connect on social media. *But be careful because this is where most people get it wrong.* They turn from networker into stalker!

We will cover more on social media later, but the main message here is just to connect and then pay attention. It's like a conversation; pay attention, listen, and be genuinely interested. When you see one of your connections post on social media, stop and read that post. Give it a thumbs up if that is appropriate. It literally takes one second to like their post and show you are paying attention. It takes one more click to share their post. If they're doing something and they've got a project going on, they've taken the time to post about it. That means that it is important to them. Click the share button and amplify their message. It costs you nothing, and it means so much to that person.

Go further, write a couple sentences about why they're awesome about the time you visited their business or some positive feedback you heard and make their day.

> *People notice people who notice them.*

If you make an effort to help them grow, they will return the favor by helping you grow. You will stay front of mind. Let me say this again:

> *People notice the people who notice them.*

Always be on the lookout for people you have made connections with. Pay attention to what is going on in their lives and ask them about it.

A few months back, I reached out to a new acquaintance I met volunteering. I invited her to connect on social media. A few weeks later, I saw that she was planning a trip to a place I have visited many times. What a great opportunity to connect and give her some details to help her plan her trip! I reached out to let her know I had gone many times to the place she was visiting and suggested some restaurants and things to do.

I was not surprised when three weeks later, I got a text with photos of her eating at the restaurant I had suggested and then more photos of her at the beach I had recommended as a great place to take her kids. We shared a laugh about a funny sign that was posted at the beach. When she returned, she reached out again to say thanks for the suggestions. From that, a relationship has continued to blossom.

If you're going to go to a restaurant and it was really amazing, take a minute and go home and write a review. Share why it was amazing. Tweet it. Put a photo on Instagram. It costs you literally nothing but a few moments, and it is way more effective than paid advertising. When you increase other people's social credit, you increase your own social credit.

The formula is really simple. Get involved, be genuine, pay attention, be helpful, and celebrate common interests together.

Notes

CHAPTER 8 - NAVIGATING SOCIAL MEDIA

*"The most successful marketer
becomes part of the lives of their
followers. They follow back. They
wish happy birthday. They handle
problems their customers have with
products or services. They grow
their businesses and brands by
involving themselves in their own
communities."*
~ Marsha Collier

Let's talk more about social media for a minute. The temptation on social media is to talk about your business and what you can offer. Instead, what you really want to do is to showcase the authenticity that makes you human. That is where connections are built.

For me, that thing is my love of animals.

I love everything about animals, and I have lots of them. I have dogs. I have cats. I have chickens. I even have goats. And even though my social media pages are business pages, I share a lot about my animals on those pages. When I have newborn baby goats in the spring, I share a video clip of them, freshly-born, trying to stand their little legs shaking, and the wonder of that new life. I share pics of myself in my gumboots mucking out stalls or bottle-feeding baby lambs because that represents my true authentic self. When my new baby chicks hatch, you can guarantee there will be videos of fuzzy little baby chicks on my feed, whether it's Instagram or Twitter, Facebook or Tik Tok.

Most of my clients, colleagues, friends, and family look forward to the pictures and appreciate them because I am not constantly spamming them with businesses and they get to know the real me. They get to see the authentic side of who I really am.

Obviously, I have business posts on there. Don't get me wrong. But the ratio is like 90/10. 90% personal, "real me" content, and 10% business content.

Even when it's business, it is chock full of valuable little tidbits that are helpful to my readers rather than generic copy written by someone who doesn't know me. I include video blogs, advice, and updates delivered by me.

I call that 10% the icing on the cake and the other 90% is you, you are the cake. Imagine you love icing, love it more than anything and you are out shopping for icing. If you came to my store and I served you a big slab of just icing, you would take a few bites and then push it away. It would be too rich. That's the same thing that happens when you only give people business content, even if they are looking for what you offer, too much is too much. They just need a sprinkle!

Think of social media as a piece of cake. It should be 90% cake (you) and 10% icing (your business). 90% of the time you want to be posting about yourself, your community, things you are passionate about, and what you are involved in. Don't just post about yourself; include posts about other people's businesses. Every post should be made with the intent to make someone smile or to elevate someone else's business or organization.

Don't feed someone an icing cake!

On social media, I have a nickname that helps people remember me. I call myself "Mortgage Monica." The alliteration helps people remember me.

When I do a video blog, I introduce myself as "Mortgage Monica," and I keep the video under 45 seconds where possible. I ensure that the content is helpful or funny or both. If you can think of a tagline or nickname for yourself, it will help people remember you.

Let me illustrate this with a story. Last year, I took my baby goats to get their vaccines and their checkups. I got to the vet clinic, dropped them off, and came back later. When I picked them up, the technician told me how popular they had been and how more than one client knew exactly who they were. One lady was sitting in the waiting room when the technician came out to get something with my goat in her arms.

One of the other clients was sitting there in the waiting room with a pet. She immediately recognized my goat! The client exclaimed, "Oh my gosh, that's Mortgage Monica's goat, Butterscotch! I recognize her from Instagram."

So even though I wasn't even there, I became part of a conversation. And because Mortgage Monica is my tagline, I am easy to remember. Someone else asked if they could snap a photo. When he went home, he posted it on Instagram but he didn't tag me or mention my name or anything. What's interesting is that, within about five minutes of his posting, someone commented, "Oh my goodness. That's Mortgage Monica's goat, Butterscotch. I love that goat. I love her little hooves."

There are lots of ways you can use this tool. Post the new recipe you tried out, the new bakery you discovered, or some new hobby you're trying — things that are authentic to you. 10% of the time, you're going to sprinkle in a little bit of business. But if all you do is make business posts, your readers will feel that they are being spammed. They will start to tune that noise out by skipping over any posts that starts with your name. Next, they will unfollow you.

Once that happens, the connection is lost and all of your work to build a connection was in vain. People are no longer interested because you sound like a taker instead of a giver. Givers give of themselves of their time with authenticity to connect with others. And people want to read their posts. They want to get to know them on a personal level. If you're a taker, then you're spamming people with business posts and they will see right through you.

On that same subject, let's talk about what not to do.

So, here's what I see people doing — and it really, really frustrates me. It kind of actually angers me when it happens to me. Someone will send me a friend request. I'll have a look at it and think, "Do I know this person? Do we have contacts in common?" Then I see that we've got fifty mutual friends. So that gives them a degree of credibility. So, I accepted their friend request, but within 20 minutes, they messaged me offering to sell me their services. One lady sent me a friend request and I accepted.

But I thought, "Okay, I'll see what this is all about." Within five minutes, she sent me a message asking if she could send me a video that would showcase her services, asking if I might be interested in buying what she has to sell. <u>Unfriended</u>!!!

This is like the vacuum salesperson coming up to your door. This is much worse than a cold call. This is like a freezing call. You're having a nice, relaxed day. You're sipping your coffee. You're enjoying yourself. There's a knock at the door. You open it up, and there's someone trying to sell you something immediately. They might have the absolute best product in the world and deliver the best pitch in the world. They might have something that you actually need and/or want. But they have broken the social contract by invading your space. There's no connection. As a result, you immediately say you're not interested and shut the door.

This happens on social media too. If you message someone without getting to know them, without building a connection first, they're going to unfollow you. They're going to block you. They're going to be pissed off.

Is it ever okay? Can you message people at some point? Yes. Once you've really gotten to know them, it's acceptable to make your pitch, but only after you have really displayed who you really are and have formed a solid connection. If you show legitimate interest in their business or maybe left a great review or shared a post or used their services, then it is okay to <u>occasionally</u> send a message about business. Even then, the touch is a gentle one:

Hey, I've got this little event coming up next week. If you're interested, drop me a note.

But if that's the first thing you do, you are going to ostracize yourself. Social media should not be a place where you go to do a hard sell.

It's a place where people get to see who you are and get to know you authentically without a bunch of pressure to buy your service — without feeling like they're in your shop every time you post. You want them to feel like they're in your living room — like you're sitting with them on your back deck having a barbecue. It's an opportunity to invite people into your life and get to know you. That is the new face of media: personal, authentic, engaging.

This approach naturally and organically leads to sales. Fully more than 90% of my business comes from social media, but I don't solicit business on social media. But I do share my authentic self there.

Let me illustrate this further by telling you about the time a spaghetti squash blew up in my oven. Yes, it's a true story. One time, I was cooking spaghetti squash in the oven, and I forgot to poke a hole in it for the steam to come out. It blew up, and there was literally spaghetti squash from one end of the kitchen to the other. It was a disaster. I snapped a picture with the caption "how not to cook spaghetti squash."

This happened almost 6 years ago. Just last year I ran into someone at an event, and they pulled their phone out and said, "OMG! I have to show you something. I still have that photo of your spaghetti squash mishap on my phone because I thought it was so funny. Whenever I'm having a bad day, I pull it out and laugh and remind myself that at least I am not cleaning up burst spaghetti squash!"

Mostly, people get to know me. The rest of the time I sprinkle in just a little bit of business stuff — just enough to show that I know what I'm talking about and to remind them that the mortgage industry is the industry I'm in. I let them know that I can be of service to them. Sure enough, when the time comes that they're looking for a service I offer, they remember me and pick up the phone or send me a message on social media.

The interesting thing is that people I have never met feel like they already know me because they have seen me or heard me already on social media.
I haven't met them yet, but they act like we have met a dozen times already because, in a way, we have. They know all about me. They have seen me with great hair and with messy hair, admitting mistakes and celebrating victories, hatching chicks, and birthing goats.

They know me on a surprisingly personal level before we even meet. Video is phenomenal. Clients will come in and I've never met them in my life, but they are already on a level of near friendship because they are familiar with my life.

There's this sense of already being part of my family, of my network because they've seen me on video. They've heard me talk from listening to my podcast. Even though I might be meeting them for the first time, *they are not meeting me for the first time*. That is how we leverage social media — not to sell people stuff, but to create familiarity and to build our community.

You can do this without ever leaving your house, walking around shaking hands, or handing out business cards. All that is required is that you must post consistently and post authentically. By consistently, I mean, at least twice a week and a variety of different things. By authentically, I mean sharing your real life.

That said, it is important to decide what degree of distance you want to maintain. You might share photos of your pets but you may choose not to share photos of your kids, or you might share both. You might share your philosophy but not your politics. You might share something funny but not anything crazy, rude, or hurtful. Never ever post a negative. Do not air your dirty laundry on social media. It is a turnoff and will backfire. Don't be that person who has a fight with their spouse or their kids and then uses social media to passive aggressively complain about it.

People see right through that. They see what you're doing. Subconsciously, they learn to fear you as a loose cannon.

They think, "Wow, someday she might do that to me. If she'll say that about her family member, what will she say about me? If she thinks that about ____, what does she think about me?" That person will likely never be your customer. They don't trust you.

When you get personal, wild, political, or combative on social media, it makes people afraid to do business with you. You appear unpredictable and unstable. Some people recommend that if you have negative posts, rants, or times when you're just pissed right off, go ahead and type it out if you need to. But leave the message there in your drafts folder for the night, but then delete it in the morning. *You will always regret a negative rant. It never reflects well on you.*

If you can, though, don't even type it. Quite a few people have accidentally posted something they intended to delete. Once it's posted, you might think you can delete it. But it is out there in some form forever. People can save it with a screenshot. As the old saying goes, "Write it, regret it." And, even if you take it down from your social media page, the person who reads it will remember and associate that negativity with you forever.

Something that one of my podcast guests, Ut Yue, shared with me on one of my first episodes stuck with me, she said:

> *"Be careful of the toes you step on today because they may be connected to the ass you kiss tomorrow."*

And it's true. Be careful who you post negatively about. Be careful who you rant about. Be careful who you freak out at and how you conduct yourself in the world, because people remember those moments and they remember them forever. Just remember that your goal is to someday make those people your clients. It might be a co-worker or a future colleague. So, treat everyone with the same kindness and the consideration that you would want to be treated with. Every day, every moment, these things you reflect on you. It's an opportunity to build your network. And you can build it in a good way, or you can build it in a bad way. I recommend you always opt for the positive.

If you have nothing positive to say about someone, say nothing; walk away from the negative. Stick with kind, uplifting, and caring posts if you want social media to help you build your business. Remember, this is your community — your neighborhood. If you blow it up, your house could come down too.
Always ask if what you are posting is something you would want to read, if it serves others, or if it only serves your agenda.

It bears repeating <u>again</u>:

people notice people who notice
them.

People whose posts you comment on, like, share, review, and shout out are going to notice that. And when it's time for them to do business, you are going to be one of the people they reach out to with the hopes of doing business with you.

Why? You are one of the people who supported them, And, in turn, you're creating this sense of reciprocity where they want to return that favor. They want to do for you what you did for them.

If you're going to post about your business on social media, be unique, and create your own content. I suggest you do some of it as a video blog. Don't post some generic article that your marketing company gave you to post. Turn on your camera. The most original things you have are your face and your voice. So, hit the record button and just begin by saying, "Hey, my name is _____. Today I want to tell you ….."

An example might look like this:

Hey, Mortgage Monica here. Hope everyone's having a great day. Just wanted to let you know that interest rates have dropped and the market's heating up. If you have questions, give me a call."

It can be just that super simple, super quick. You're not selling something. Rather, you are inviting people to reach out if they need more information and positioning yourself as the expert in your market.

So, let's recap that:

- **Number one:** be your authentic self. Show who you really are and do that with stories, videos, and photos to share interesting, engaging and funny content. Share that silly viral video you saw, or an inspiring quote, something that connects people that makes them feel warm and fuzzy.

- **Number two:** elevate others. Spend time building up other people by leaving a positive review for a business you visited. Talk about the great book you just read or share a friend's post. If you're going to an event, you should be sharing that. When the event is over and if it was awesome, say so.

- It provides valuable information for others who might want to go and it is valuable for the event organizers and it grows your community. You can say, "I'm going to this event. I'm looking forward to it. I hope to see you there too." people that didn't know about it are going to be made aware and think about going. Organizers are going to notice that you took the time to share their event.

- **Number three:** remember to sprinkle a little business over it all... but just a little because you can have too much of a thing. If you're afraid of videos then don't do a live video, do a recorded video. The wonderful thing about recorded video is you can tape yourself over and over and over again until you are satisfied with it. You can do it a hundred times if you want.

It doesn't have to be fancy; it just needs to be authentic Go on zoom, start a new meeting, choose a decent background, hit record, and just start talking. You can do those 500 times until you find the perfect clip. Once you do, share it. The more times you do it, the more comfortable you will be and the better you'll get at it.

Remember the bitter coffee that became my daily necessity? When you first see yourself on video, you will hate it. Don't obsess over it. Make another one. With each recording, it will feel more natural. One day, it will feel like an old hat and you will laugh and how you used to struggle with it. It is kind of like jumping into a pool for the first time of the day.

The water is cold. You don't want to ease in. You must jump in the deep end. Suddenly the water feels warm and you are off swimming happily. Videos are the same way. Keep at it. When you have a version you love, save it and upload it to social media.

Notes

CHAPTER 9 - SOWING SEEDS AND ORGANIC GROWTH

*"Successful people do what
unsuccessful people are not willing
to do. Don't wish it were easier;
wish you were better.*
~ Jim Rohn

When you start out as an entrepreneur or in a sales role, you can choose to be a farmer or a hunter. This is metaphorical, so take it with a grain of salt. Let's assume that hunters are always on the prowl for their next meal. They don't spend a lot of time planning for the future. When they are hungry, they just go get dinner. A farmer on the other hand is always planning for the future. They care about the land and the resources, and they know the time and effort they put in now will pay off later. They grow their food slowly and store what they grow for the changing of the seasons when nothing grows.

The reality is that most people start off in the hunter category because there's literally nothing else available. Here's the thing about hunters though: every day they must go out and look for food. They have to catch it. If they kill it, they must hide it from the other predators that want to take away their bounty. A kill might last them a few days, but as soon as it's gone, they have to get out and do it again. It's exhausting, it's tiring, and it wears you down.

If we look long-term at the anecdotal differences between hunters and farmers from a sales perspective, we see an interesting trend. In the first couple of years, a hunter-style salesperson sees their sales move in an upward trajectory. They rocket upwards because every day they bring in food (sales); but then something surprising happens. Somewhere about the three-year mark, that starts to taper off and often they actually start to go down because they run out of resources and energy.

They don't have anymore friends and family to tap, having exhausted both their inner circle and outer circle.

It's a lot of work to go out and look for prey every day and, at some point, you simply start to run out. Metaphorically, they run out of customers because they're not thinking about a product that's going to come back to them. They're just thinking about what they are going to eat today. If you are a family of foxes, you raid every chicken coop in the area until there is no chicken left to eat. You must eventually move on to a new area or choose a new food source.

The same thing goes for entrepreneurs that only use a hunter model. You'll see them change frequently from company to company, industry to industry. Maybe they were selling cars, and now they're selling cell phones. Perhaps they were doing life insurance and now they're doing extended health insurance enrollments. This is because they have hit everyone they know in the community and have nothing to fall back once those resources are gone. Once they have run out of customers or reputation, they either need to move to a new product or they need to move geographically to a completely new area.

In the short term, it is a good idea to have some hunter traits just to get some sales under your belt. It is fine to go out there and actively look for clients that you can close today. Long-term, though, this will not create a steady stream of business. Meanwhile, let's look at what those farmer types are doing.

Remember how the graph for the hunters went straight up and then started to level out or even go down about the 3-year mark? What about farmers? If we look at that graph, we will see that farmers may struggle initially, they might actually lose some money in that first six months to a year. They'll have a very slow start but long-term, instead of going straight upwards, they consistently curve up and up and up. They get to a point where they literally have to do no sales-related activities except show up and do a good job. The phone rings, the emails come in, and the clients show up at the door because they've been planting seeds all year. All they need to do now is harvest their crops.

Let me give you an example of this. When my husband and I were in our 20s and were looking to buy our first home, we sought out a realtor on the recommendation of other people.

We were so excited, but we had almost no money and the houses that we could afford to buy were all in terrible condition or sold before we had a chance to make an offer. We got to the point where we were just ready to buy anything. One evening, we took a drive out to look at yet another place and were pleasantly surprised to find a cute little house with an acre of property. It was a lovely little yard and a beautiful house. We just wanted to have it. We told the agent (Rob Nygren), "Write the deal! Let's do it today."

Had that realtor been exclusively a hunter, he would've pulled out his pen and paper and written that offer.

He would have had that file done and been paid by the end of the month. He wasn't a hunter, though. He got this kind of funny, pained look on his face. He gestured for us to follow him over to one part of the yard where he pointed at the lid of the well:

"I want you to look at this. Do you know what this is?"

My husband said, "Yeah, that's the lid for the well. It's a rural property."

Then he said, "You're right, but now look over here."

He pointed to something else on the ground about six feet away. It was another lid. "Do you know what this is?"

My husband and I looked at each other kind of puzzled.

He said, "This is a lid for the septic tank." He paused for a minute to let that sink in and then he asked, "Do you want to live in a house where your well is 6 feet from your septic? I don't know about you, but if I was going to raise children, I would want to know that my water supply was safer than that."

My husband and I were surprised that he took the time to care about us more than making a sale.

He said, "Look, I know you guys are excited. I know you've been disappointed because some of the houses you've looked at have sold, but just wait!

The right house will come along. It doesn't have to be this house. We will keep looking and find the right house for you. It may take us six months. Maybe it'll be a year. But you are going to live in this place for a long time. You're gonna invest a lot of money, and you need to make the right decision."

What was he doing? He was planting seeds of trust and integrity and honesty. Six months later, we decided to go looking again, but there was still a shortage of houses and money was tight. The only house that we could find that we could afford was in a little community called Cumberland BC. At that time, because it was such a tiny community, it was basically a village.

Since the house was not located in the big urban centre, the big banks and credit unions were not interested in lending money for mortgages there. Instead of getting discouraged we found ourselves a mortgage broker and, after a lot of declines, she found us a mortgage. The kicker was the only mortgage she could get approved was a private mortgage.... at 14% interest.

Thrilled that we were finally approved and determined that we would eat Kraft dinners and work extra hours if that was what it took to get into a house of our own finally, we called up our realtor. I gave him the news that we were approved for the mortgage and told him to write the offer.

"Wow," he said, "you got a mortgage in Cumberland. "I thought it was only cash purchasers or private lenders there."

"Oh yes," I said. "It's a private lender, but we got approved. It's all good."

"A private lender?" he asked. "What's the interest rate on that?"

I paused at that point as even I realized how bad it sounded out loud, "Well, it's 14%, but we think we can make it work. We can both work extra hours, and I don't really need a fancy vehicle."

This time there was a big pause at the other end of the line. "Rob? Are you still there?"

Finally, he spoke. "Here's the thing," he said. These are tough times in real estate, and I could really use the commission, but I can't let you buy this house. You are going to be house poor making payments at that rate, and it's not even that nice of a house. If you were my kids, I would tell you to wait. Keep saving your money, and the right house will come along."

Again, if he had been a hunter, he would have pounced on this commission, he would have written the offer and gotten paid and not thought about it again. But he knew something it would take me years to learn: sooner or later we would have realized our mistake and we would associate that mistake with him.

We would regret it, and it would leave a bad taste in our mouths. The likelihood of our doing business with him again in the future would have been slim to none.

Instead, he again planted seeds of integrity, honesty, kindness, transparency. He didn't eat that day, but he planted seeds that would grow crops for decades. Six months later when we started looking again, we found the house of our dreams. He was there to help us write an offer and get us the best deal possible.

Four years after that, when we upgraded to a bigger home, guess who we called? And five years after that when we decided to convert that home to a revenue property and buy a new one, guess who we called? Same guy. Now that I am a mortgage professional and I have an opportunity to refer my own clients to a realtor I trust, who do you think I send those referrals too?

By planting seeds instead of hunting, by delaying gratification and nurturing a relationship, and doing the right thing, he has harvested that crop many times over rather than just cashing a paycheck once.

When I first started out as a mortgage broker it was hard. I was fully on commission, and I was starving. I was bleeding money. I had no files, no prospect of files, and I had office rent, association dues, advertising, and other expenses to pay. I knew it was a long game. I knew I had to build relationships, get good at my job, and build trust before I would get clients.

So, I decided to focus on giving rather than receiving. I helped other brokers with their files, I volunteered in my community, I went to conferences, and I made sure I was ready so that when I got a "real client," I would be able to provide them the highest level of service possible.

Finally, after months of no business, my phone rang and it was a couple who wanted to refinance their home to take some money out for renovations. Their mortgage was not up for renewal for a couple years, but they didn't want to wait. I looked at their documents, their current mortgage, and their goals. I knew I could take their mortgage to a new lender, get them a new mortgage, and earn a commission on the whole amount.

I also knew that if I did that, they would have to pay a penalty, legal fees, and appraisal fees. It could cost them as much as $10,000 just to borrow $30,000 for renovations. I would not just get paid on the extra $30,000, I would get paid on the full mortgage amount of $500,000. This was a big commission for me at that time that would have helped me pay off all the bills I had racked up waiting to earn a paycheck at my new career. It would also make me look productive at my office instead of the new girl who was eight months in without a single paying client.

If I wanted to be a hunter, I would have gotten that mortgage done and signed and walked away with a big fat paycheck. The problem is I knew that there was another option for them.

I knew that if I just sent them back to their own bank, they could add a $30,000 line of credit onto their existing mortgage with no legal fees, no penalty, and no appraisal.

I told them the truth — that we could take their mortgage to another lender and get them the money they wanted, but it was an ineffective and expensive way to do it and not in their best interest. I recommended they go directly to their own bank.

"But we hate our bank," they said. "They treat us like crap and we want to leave anyway. We will just pay the penalty. We want to work with you"

I said "Do you hate them $10,000 worth? Because that's what it's going to cost you to do this today. Honestly just go back to your bank. I will tell you exactly what to ask for. I will even give you the name of a bank rep who will be a pleasure to deal with and who will look after you carefully and professionally. Then in two years when your mortgage is up for renewal, come see me, and I will look after you. We will get you with a better lender at a better rate and we can make sure that you are never stuck with a penalty like this again in the future. But not today. Today, you should go back to your bank and save yourself $10k."

They left my office grateful for the advice and for the introduction to a very competent branch rep who helped them get the funds they needed with no extra fees. When they left my office, I phoned another new broker colleague and told him what I had done.

"Are you bleeping crazy?!?" he said. "Why would you do that, you are literally bleeding money and you send them out the door? That was a $7000 commission. What's wrong with you?"

"I guess I'm a farmer not a hunter," I said. "I could not do the wrong thing when the right thing was so obvious."

"But they didn't even like their bank! You were doing them a favor."

"No, I really would not have been and we both know it."

I headed home for the day wondering how I was going to pay that month's office rent and broker fees. The next morning my phone rang, and it was the couple's friend. They were looking for a new house and needed approval right away. They wanted to deal with someone honest who would look out for their best interests, and they were told they should call me.

I completed that transaction which was a huge purchase and an even bigger commission than their friends would have been. Their realtor was so pleased with how smoothly it went that he sent me his next new home buyer a week later, and they referred their parents to me. From that day forward, I was a busy broker.

Files started to just flow in organically from all over. Just as soon as one closed, another referral would come in.

Yes, some months were quieter and some months I was totally slammed but, with every transaction, I planted seeds and those seeds continue to grow and be harvested.

Every decision you make, every interaction you have with someone, every conversation is an opportunity to plant a seed and grow a beautiful garden that you can harvest year after year. Choose your crops wisely, nurture them, water them, and care for them, and as the years go by, you can enjoy the bounty of your hard work for decades. This doesn't just apply to files and sales; this also applies to life, friendships, and family members.

Look for places where you can add value to other people's lives. Do the right things. Plant honesty, plant kindness, plant integrity, and enjoy the rewards of your efforts day after day, decade after decade.

Notes

CHAPTER 10 - DON'T COUNT YOUR CHICKENS BEFORE THEY HATCH

*"Goodness is about character —
integrity, honesty, kindness,
generosity, moral courage, and the
like. More than anything else, it is
about how we treat other people."*
~ Dennis Prager

When you're hungry, just starting out, and not making much money, it's easy to get wrapped up in the question of how big your paycheck is going to be. New entrepreneurs or sales professionals will look at a job or a client and the first thing that they calculate in their mind is how much they are going to get paid on the file in front of them.

Maybe it's the guy at the Electronics Store showing people different TVs. But his mind is locked on one question: which one of these is going to pay me the most? Or maybe it's a Real Estate Agent and, as she's showing houses, she is asking them about their budget because she is roughly calculating the commission on her head and spending it.

As a mortgage broker this is something I see happen all the time, even with really ethical brokers who really care about their clients. They can't help themselves. A client walks in needing a mortgage and, as soon as they hear the amount, they start calculating that commission. And it completely distracts them from their mission to serve their customers.

When a person's income fluctuates from month to month, it is normal to get excited about income. The problem with this is that they are counting their chickens before they hatch. If you find yourself in this position, be careful.

First of all, it takes you away from the present moment, leaving you distracted. You are no longer focused and listening to the client you're there to serve.

You're off in some future space — a future you can't control and that hasn't happened yet.

Besides, you are already committing yourself to an outcome. You are thinking that $2000 will pay the rent this month or replace the washing machine that broke down last week. As a result, you are not doing what is best for the client that is right in front of you since your need is competing with what is best for them.

Pre-spending money you don't have and haven't earned yet almost never ends well.

Remember when we talked about hunter versus farmer mentality? As soon as you focus on how much that paycheck is going to be, you've just thrown all your seeds away. You're now in the mode of the hunter and you're focusing on your customer as your prey. Your mind is locked on what you're going to eat today instead of the crops you can grow in the future if you ensure you serve your customer well.

It taints the entire process. Those thoughts are like a cancer that will seep into your file and kill it. Or, if you get this file, it will be the last one with this customer. You will lose their future business and many referrals they might have led you to.

When a client walks in, they come in as a blank canvas on which you can paint anything. It can be beautiful. You have the opportunity to use all the colors, all the designs, all the creativity you want to make your experience with them whatever painting will be best.

But then, you started calculating your paycheck. When you did, you started to decide what that painting was going to look like before the clients had even given you their vision. That takes the painting and turns it into something grotesque that will give you that paycheck, but may not result in the right outcome for them.

What's worse is that this kind of thinking makes you a little needy, because your focus is on money rather than the virtues that make a business thrive. You're thinking about where you're going to spend your money, so you commit to getting this file done, no matter what. That makes you too hungry and desperate.

Remember we talked about the human instinct and how it gives us clues we can't explain? Your client may not know you are seeing them as a cash register, but they will feel it.

When you're calculating your commission in your head, clients can see it, they can hear it in your voice and in your mannerisms, and it repels them and makes them uncomfortable.

They can feel the vibe in the room shift to a dark place. All of a sudden you go from nice, calm, casual, and helpful to tense, rushed, and needy. You go from "how can I help you" to "how can you help me."

Consciously or subconsciously, you push things on them, introducing your own biases into their transaction. The client senses the pressure even if all of your words are right. They start to retreat because they can feel your prey drive kicking in like a predator stalking its prey. As the metaphorical saliva drips from your lips, they see themselves skinned and cooked on the dinner plate. You're not a wolf stalking a deer, but essentially, in terms of evolution, you go back to your wolf nature, thinking about that commission and trying to make it work any way you can.

They might go through with the deal because they feel pressured. But they won't come back or tell anyone anything good about you. Just the opposite. They become negative advertising for you as they share with friends and family to stay away.

I remember a mortgage broker once calling me because she was struggling with a file. She said, "I need your help getting something to work.

It's the most amazing deal. It's going to be a $900,000 refinance. My commission on this is going to be over $10,000."

Right away, I thought to myself, "I don't think I'd be calculating that commission yet if I were you. The only reason you're calling me is you're having trouble getting this file done and you are reaching out for extra help because you have hit a wall somewhere. You've lost sight of your ultimate purpose: servicing your clients' needs."

She went on and on telling me about some of the challenges of the file:

"Well, here's the first challenge: The thing is, for me to refinance them, they have to leave their current bank. They have a $500,000 mortgage, and they need another $400,000 because they want to help their kids buy a house and do some renovations.

The problem is, if they break their current mortgage, the penalty is about $40,000."

"Have you considered that maybe switching lenders right now isn't the best thing for them?" I asked. "Maybe you should tell them to go back to their bank and get a line of credit or a second mortgage at the same bank so they don't pay the penalty on the first. Why don't you tell them to go back to their bank and do a blend and extend? It would save them a ton of money."

She replied, "Yeah, I already talked to their bank, and they're just giving me some crap about doing the best thing for the client, but I <u>am</u> doing the best thing for the client! They hate that bank and they want to leave! I am just trying to help them."

"Okay," I said as calmly as I could. "I get that they hate their bank, but do they hate them $40,000 worth? I mean, the term is up in a year. You can tell them to stay for this year and then next year, you can move them when there is not penalty."

"I get that," she fired back. "But it's a $900,000 file, I'd like to find a way to make it work."

I had a hard time keeping my inside voice inside. "So, is this really about the client? Or is this about you needing to get paid?"

She got a little defensive. "Well, of course I want to do the best thing for the client, but it's a $900,000 file!"

Several times in the course of five minutes, she mentioned that it was a $900,000 file as if that mattered one bit. She had become the wolf and the hunt was on. She was calculating the commission and could not be bothered to be swayed by ethics. She was determined to get this done and she didn't care how she was going to get it done or at what cost to her clients or her future business prospects with them.

She talked herself into the idea that she was doing the best thing for the client because they didn't like their bank. She had told herself that the .5% in interest they would save with a new lender was enough of a savings to make up for the $40,000 plus in fees that they would have to pay out to get a slightly lower rate and a new lender.

The reality is that she had probably already spent that commission in her mind. She was already paying off that credit card or had mentally placed herself on a plane to a nice vacation; she didn't want to give it up now when it was so close. I followed up with her a month later to hear the end of the story, which was that her clients started to sense that there was a shark in the water. They thought about it and realized that $40,000 is a lot of money to throw away.

As they started to backpedal, she went on the attack saying (and believing) things like "just give me a chance, I can get this done. I can get a lower rate. It's going to be better for you. You don't have to deal with this bank that you hate, they are just going to lock you into a new penalty if you go back to them, look at how they have treated you."

Her verbal language and body language gave them all the reasons they needed to question the wisdom of the file. She also subtly implied that she had put a lot of time into their file and they somehow owed her. She didn't say those words outright, but hinted at it in an attempt to make them feel guilty.

Without intending to, she alienated them. They ended up deciding it was best to stay where they were. This put her on the defense, causing her to argue with her own client about why they should make a bad decision.

She was very disappointed. I could tell by her tone and words how it all shook down:

"They decided it wasn't worth it and they basically ended up ghosting me and dropping all contact. I can't believe it! I spent so much time trying to help them, and they were so ungrateful. I think they went back to their old bank. I was supposed to be doing the purchase for their kids too, because they were going to use some of the money for a down payment for them. I lost their mortgage, too. I don't understand. They said they hated their bank. I was trying to do the right thing for them. People have no loyalty."

I shook my head and wished her well as I hung up the phone. The reality is she lost her ability to be loyal to her own client the minute she calculated that commission in her head and started to spend it before it was in her hands. It created fear in them.

She was in hunter mode and didn't even realize it. She wanted that money. She lost two files that day and who knows how many more that would have come from their friends, family members, and other contacts.

The wolf went hungry that day and ensured many skinny days to come!

What if she'd done something differently? What if she'd been the farmer instead? What if she'd put that commission completely aside and not thought about it? What if her focus was on the people in front of her and how she could be of service to them? What if her only goal was the right thing for them?

Yes, she still would have lost that first mortgage because she would've sent them back to their bank. But the upside is how she would have looked in their eyes. They would have been shocked and impressed that she walked away from a commission because it was the right thing to do. She would have cultivated trust, and that trust would have resulted in the kids' mortgage. She would have at least gotten half the paycheck instead of none of it. And maybe she would have gotten some other referrals. She would have planted seeds. Then for the next 5, 10, 15 years, she could have had their business anytime they thought about a refinance or a new purchase.

Notes

CHAPTER 11 – EXCUSE ME, BUT YOUR BIAS IS SHOWING

"While you judge me by my outward appearance, I am silently doing the same to you, even though there's a ninety percent chance that in both cases our assumptions are wrong.
~ Richelle E. Goodrich

A few years ago, a woman in sweatpants and a baseball cap walked into a swanky Switzerland boutique. The upscale establishment sold only high-end purses starting at $5000. The woman pointed to a $38,000 Tom Ford crocodile skin purse hanging on the display and asked the clerk to take it down so she could see it. The clerk refused, telling the woman that she couldn't afford anything in the store and suggested that she should leave. "Ok," the woman replied before walking out of the shop. By the way, that woman was Oprah Winfrey — the billionaire!

Who knows if the clerk was biased against her because of her clothing, because she was Black, because she came in alone? There is no way to tell what was in the clerk's heart. But we know what wasn't in her wallet: her commission. There is no way to know what Oprah would have purchased that day. But it's fair to say she could have bought everything in the store — and then bought the store!

Another huge mistake is to introduce bias into a transaction and treat someone differently based on how they look, how much money they make, or how much money they plan to spend. I talked to a car salesman once about an experience like this. He told me about a woman who came onto the lot to buy a car. She was just wearing jeans and an old t-shirt. So, he asked her what her budget was. She said "Well, it's for my kid. I need a $3,000 car that will get her from home to school and back without any huge issues. It doesn't have to be pretty — just reliable."

Immediately he calculated the commission in his head and realized he wasn't going to make much money from this sale. He wasn't about to spend a bunch of time to sell a $3,000 car. It was near the end of the day, and he was thinking about going home, putting his feet up, and watching a game with his buddies. So, he passed the prospect off to a new sales guy who was keen just to get some experience and a little bit of money. The new guy didn't care about the commission. He just wanted a shot to get in front of a customer and do a good job. He went out of his way to create an amazing experience for the woman.

He found a great economical car in good condition. A month after the purchase, he followed up with her by asking "How's your car working out? How's everything going?" He treated this $3k client the same way he would a $50k client. He acted with integrity and made her feel safe and cared for and valued. He was more concerned that her daughter loved the car and that it was in good repair. What happens?

She was thrilled with the level of service. Just hearing his voice reminded her of the positive experience she had with him. She said, "Thanks for helping me find a car for my kid. That was my most important priority last month. Now that that's sorted out, I need a new van for my business and my budget is about $80,000."

BAM!

That's what happens when you don't look at the commission, when you treat every client like your best client, and when you focus on providing the best experience you can. He treated sale A, the same as sale B. He treated customer A the same as customer B. It's just like the lesson your mom or your dad or teacher probably taught you when they said, "Everyone is equal. It doesn't matter what they do for a living or the color of their skin."

The size of the commission should not dictate the level of service that you provide. Never! NEVER! **NEVER!** Don't calculate your commissions in your head while talking to a customer or working on their transaction.
Don't daydream about what you will spend the money on? Put it out of your mind until the transaction is done and completed.

Regardless of whether you make $1, $10,000, or zero on a file, you want to mentally be in the space where you are planting seeds, building a relationship, and giving the absolute best service experience possible. Never leave your customers feel like they are a means to an end for you. It's the opposite. Make sure your transaction is based on integrity, transparency, and great service levels, because those are the things that are going to grow your business.

In Thomas Stanley's book, *The Millionaire Next Door*, he shatters many of the myths we hold in our minds about what millionaires look like, who they are, how they live, and where they live. His survey of hundreds of millionaires showed that a millionaire could be living in your neighborhood.

They don't dress in the latest styles or worry themselves over name brand clothing. They might even be driving a modest car. They made good financial decisions so that they can have the things they really want. When they get ready to make a purchase, they are financially prepared to close the deal.

Treat every client like they are worth your time, your attention, and your follow up. Trust that they are worth it no matter how things look at first glance and no matter if you're selling them a pencil or selling them an entire office suite. They will feel it if you are prejudging them. They will sense it and they will react to it.

After you make the sale and get that paycheck, you can celebrate it. But wait until it is in your hand and you know that there is a happy customer on the other end of that transaction who is also celebrating — because they are happy with their purchase and have no regrets. Then, and only then, you can think about where you're going to spend it. You did it! You put your clients needs ahead of your own and it paid off. You treated your client like you would a family member.

The moral of the story is clear: Do the right thing and the money will follow.

Notes

CHAPTER 12 - SILENCE IS DEADLY, SO COMMUNICATE

"Not following up is the same as filling your bathtub without first putting the stopper in the drain."
~ Michelle Moore

We learned in a previous chapter that being too eager or too hungry introduces stress into the equation and will scare away your potential clients. But this works in reverse also. Failure to communicate creates a different kind of stress.

I want you for a minute to think about a time when you were waiting to hear back about something important. Maybe you just had a fantastic job interview and were waiting for the callback to let you know you got the job. Or perhaps you applied for a loan and the banker said they would let you know once they reviewed everything. Three days pass and then four and then a week goes by. As that time passes, your mind creates its own story about what is happening because it doesn't know what's going on. It starts to fill in the blanks with its own ideas.

Instead of imagining the best-case scenarios, your brain immediately goes to the worst-case scenarios. You start thinking things like "they didn't like me" or "obviously I didn't get the job" without actually knowing what the reality is.

Waiting for a response has a negative effect on both parties. If you're the job interviewer and you have a huge pool of candidates to get through, you can easily get overloaded. If you are slow to call back your best candidates and you take too long to process everyone, you might find that, by the time you actually get to the point where you're scheduling second interviews, half of those candidates may have already applied elsewhere and gotten another job simply because you didn't communicate with them.

Had you built communication into your process and sent out an email saying, "We're working through our list of candidates. You are still under consideration. Please be patient and we will be in touch with you by X-date," then those candidates might not have gone elsewhere. It's a loss for you of quality prospects, and it's a loss for the candidate because they no longer have a shot at working for your company.

Same with that Mortgage Broker. Maybe they got swamped and didn't have time to look at the file yet. Or maybe they were leaving on holiday the next day and forgot to let their clients know that there would be a delay. If they had told clients in advance or checked in with them, the expectation would have been and there would not be any stress.

It is simply unacceptable to wait two weeks to get back to someone if they were expecting to hear from you in a few days. The client starts to worry. They assume their application was denied and that you don't bother to call back the denials. So, they go elsewhere. That new broker is on her or his game and gets everything processed. They communicate with the client in a timely fashion. But the time you check-in with them to tell them they are approved, they are already locked in with someone else.

One of the things that I hear most from professionals is "if everything's going great there's no reason to call the client and bother them." That is one of the most damaging stories you will ever tell yourself. It doesn't matter if things are going great or if things are falling apart.

Communication is required! If you don't communicate with your client, they will have their own conversation in their head about what's happening, and I guarantee it will be completely different than any real-life story you could share with them.

People want to feel part of the process. they want to feel updated, and they want to be informed. They like to know that you are still working on their file. All it takes is a quick text or email. It can be done once a day at the end of the day so that you are not being interrupted by constant calls.

When people know what's going on and they're looped in, their stress hormones stay nice and low and they feel comfortable. Once they get annoyed, frustrated, or upset, it's tough to get them back.

When they don't know what's going on, the first thing that happens is they want to call you. Some call over and over until they get an answer. Some want to call but don't want to be annoying or bothersome. So, they just sit home and stew. This in itself causes stress because you're putting the client in the position of not wanting to bother you which is completely unfair. Of course, you want them to call you, but you're putting them in a spot where they feel like it's a problem if they do, and that creates another whole level of anxiety.

Remember back in your younger days — before we had text messages, emails, or social media — and you were waiting for a boyfriend or a girlfriend to call you? They didn't call, and you were heartbroken.

So, you'd come home and check your voicemail, or you'd pick up the phone and make sure the dial tone actually worked. You didn't want to call them because you didn't want to sound desperate, but in your mind, the lack of communication was troubling to you. In the absence of the truth, your imagination ran wild.

You told yourself all kinds of stories about how they didn't like you or what they were doing without you or who they were seeing instead of you. Sometimes those stories were true. But most of the time, something happened that kept them too busy to call. Your mind invented all the worst-case scenarios. So, when they did call you, you were either angry or sounding needy and desperate.

If they had just quickly reached and said (or wrote): "Hey, I'm thinking of you. I'm working a lot this week, but you will be on my mind. I'll talk to you in a couple of days," it would have removed all the stress from the equation. My husband and I took years to work this out in our marriage. When we were first married, he would stop at a friend's house on the way home from work and not bother to tell me. I would start to wonder where he was.

My first thought was whether he was safe or if he had an accident. Then my imagination would create other scenarios that were unflattering to him. By the time he got home, I was stressed out and angry.

He would be puzzled that I was in such a frenzy when he walked in the door. "I just stopped in to visit a friend," he would say. "It's not like you don't know where I am. What's the big deal?" But it <u>was</u> a big deal, and I didn't know anything for sure. At the time, text messaging was just a fantasy in some inventor's mind. He could not just send a quick text and, half the time, he didn't have his cell phone turned on.

The point is that not knowing can create conflict in even the most loving and close relationships.

Nowadays if either of us is stopping somewhere, we send a quick text and say we will be late. It's just being considerate and helps the other person not to have to wonder what's going on. It's taken all the stress out of our relationship.

Think of the parent whose kid is away from home for the first time. If they get a little text once or twice a day that says, "Hey, Mom! Everything's going great. I'm enjoying my classes, I'll talk to you later," then there's no worry. The parent knows everything's good. Realistically they have nothing exciting to report if everything is normal but for the person on the other end is just helpful to know that things are fine. One mother I know asks her children to just send a meme or an emoji when they wake and just before going to bed when they are away. The kids love picking a silly face or a funny pic and the mom relaxes knowing her kids are ok.

Clients are no different from your family. In fact, it may be even more critical to reach out with a client because you don't have years of history and relationship to rely on. Your mom will forgive you for not touching base. Clients won't. They need to know that everything is fine.

When I take a mortgage application from someone, I collect their documents and submit them to a lender for an approval. At that point, it is out of my hands. I cannot control how long it will be for the lender to get back to me. And the time that approval will take depends on a lot of things: how busy the lender is, if the home needs an appraisal, what type of income the applicant has, and if it's in the middle of a busy home buying season or not. It can take as little as 24 hours or as much as 4 weeks depending on the situation.

During that time, I am not stressed because I know that everything is fine. I know the file is just sitting in a queue waiting to be looked at or waiting on an appraiser to be free. I have no concerns. The problem is that my client doesn't know that even if I told them that on the day I took all of their information. They are anxious. This means much more to them than it does to me or the bank. This is their life — their home. If I don't reach out to them during those days and weeks, they start thinking about all the worst-case scenarios. They think, "Oh no, I'm not going to get approved. I'm not going to get this house. There must be a problem. Why isn't she calling me."

Sometimes they get so panicked, they actually go to another lender because they think this one's not going to approve them. They want to keep their options flowing because they don't want to lose the house.

I've talked to mortgage brokers or loan officers who have had this happen. And they have the nerve to be baffled that the client bolted and ran. They say:

"I don't get it! Everything was perfect. I got it done. I got them their approval. But when I reached out to tell them I had an approval, they had already gotten it approved elsewhere."

"What did they say when you called?" I asked.

"I asked why they would go somewhere else when I was working on their file and they told me that they were worried it wouldn't be approved in time because they hadn't heard from me."

Some business people even tell people, "If you don't hear from me, assume everything is OK." Are you joking? If people don't hear from you, I can assure you they will assume the opposite. It never fails. Lack of communication never leads to anything good.

Let me tell you what my process looks like and how it makes my clients feel calm, relaxed and well taken care of. First of all, communication starts with that first conversation when I take their documents. During that discussion, we talk about their goals and what the process is going to look like. I go over the timeline:

"Everything looks great. I've got everything I need here to get started. I just want to let you know it's an incredibly busy time in real estate and every lender is overwhelmed with applications. I am going to submit this today, but I want you to know it could take a while to get an official approval. I will check on it on a regular basis and, if anything additional is required, I will reach out to you. When I reach out to you looking for additional documents, or if I have questions, it's important that you get back to me in a timely manner so that we can keep the process moving along.

Even though I have everything I think I need, I can't read the lender's mind. Since they are lending you a lot of money, they may have additional questions. They may ask for an appraisal or an extra pay stub. They might want to know why you took that three weeks off last year. It could be almost anything that they request clarification about. I will keep you informed all along the way."

That was step one — setting the expectation of the worst-case scenario for how long it could take and what I might need from them along the way. Then, two days after that, I follow up with a quick email. I write:

"Hey! This is just a quick update to confirm that I have submitted your application and all your documents. Your file is sitting in the queue waiting to be reviewed by the lender."

If the application still hasn't been picked up two days later, I will send another email and write:

"Just letting you know that I haven't forgotten about you. I followed up on this today and the lender expects to review it on Monday. Once they have completed their review, I will let you know if anything else is required."

All through the process, I do these little check-ins so that they never have to wonder what's going on. They never have to call me because they get in the habit of expecting to hear something from me every couple of days. They never have to feel bad about wanting to call me but being worried about bothering me. This lowers their cortisol levels which helps them feel calm and relaxed, and they associate feeling calm and relaxed with me and a smooth transaction. That makes them want to come back again and again. They have a sense that they're taken care of, that I value their time, and that they are a partner in the process — not just a spectator. This ultimately is the essence of building a relationship, a relationship of trust that will create more relationships through referrals.

You see, it doesn't matter how well you build your initial relationships and how good you are at networking and getting people in the door if you don't keep the momentum going. Relationships take work whether they are personal or professional. They need continual care and attention to grow.

Networking does not stop with a transaction; it continues all the way through the lifetime of the relationship. When things go sideways, and they sometimes do, it's even more important that I communicate and communicate transparently and openly. Just like with marriages and personal relationships, if things go wrong, the best thing is to talk about them right away before they fester.

I remember being out for lunch with a commissioned salesperson once and his phone kept ringing. He kept turning it off and shaking his head.

"Do you need to pick that up," I asked. "It looks like someone's anxiously trying to reach you?" I was really surprised at his response.

"No, I don't know yet if we were able to get his unit in stock yet, so I don't want to talk to him until I have good news. It's just going to stress them out if I tell him I haven't found one yet. I know I can locate one, I just need to make a few more calls. I need a little more time."

This was absolutely the worst thing he could have done. His clients are phoning because they are feeling anxious and stressed and they need to be updated on their status. That is true even if the update is "nothing new to report."

His failure to pick up the phone was now going to increase the client's stress level and confirm his suspicion that there is something wrong. It also confirms his worst fear that he is not being taken care of.

That is the state of North American business and, I suspect, business in many places around the world. Mediocre is the new standard. People do the bare minimum. Customers walk into a transaction expecting poor service because that is what they receive wherever they go. Stellar service is now an anomaly as rare as a Bigfoot sighting.

I talked to my friend two weeks later and asked him how that file worked out:

"Well," he started. "I found the unit. But it didn't matter. People have no sense of loyalty these days. They don't respect the time it takes to get things done. By the time I called to tell them I had located one, they'd already gone somewhere else. I can't believe they did that after all the work I put into finding exactly what they wanted. What a bunch of jerks."

I just shook my head and thought, "Wow! Go look in the mirror. You are the jerk today." He couldn't understand that those clients just wanted to be included in the process whether it was good, bad, or ugly. They wanted and deserved to be updated and informed.

Had they been, they would have been loyal to the ends of the earth. However, because they were excluded, they felt left out, abandoned, and unsafe. They went to where they did feel safe — a different company, far away from that guy.

If you get nothing else out of this chapter, please get this: when things go well, communicate. When things go wrong, communicate even more.

No, you don't need to tell the client that the whole thing is going sideways and scare the crap out of them. But you do need to tell them that you're working on it. Let them know you are on the job, you are watching over their situation, and that it's going to be OK.

I once had a client who was purchasing a condo. Her mortgage paperwork was submitted but the lender came back and said that they wouldn't lend on that particular building because there were too many rentals in it. It's a silly thing, but it's just something that lenders sometimes choose to do. It was an easy solution for me just to submit it to a different lender and get an approval elsewhere, but that was going to take a couple of days. While I was in the process of submitting it to a new lender, I called the customer to deliver the news.

I could have done what most other brokers do and just submit the paperwork on the sly without informing the customer. But he deserved to know what was happening. I chose to pick up the phone, be proactive, and keep him informed. I said, "I don't have an approval yet as the lender I was hoping to use has changed their policy.

This property doesn't quite fit their requirements anymore. The good news is that I have forty other lenders to choose from. I've already reached out to one of them and they have no concerns. I'm going to submit everything to them today, and I would expect to have an approval tomorrow or the next day. I will update you either way in a couple of days."

Instead of avoiding the situation I confronted it head on and I did three things:

1. I was truthful about the fact that we didn't yet have what he needed.
2. I gave him enough information and details to satisfy his questions but not so much to scare or overwhelm him.
3. I confirmed that I was working on a solution and let him know when he could expect to hear from me again.

This works for other kinds of sales also. Let's use a car purchase as an example. A few years ago, I was looking for a new car, and the dealership I went to didn't have the exact model that I wanted. They said they would try and find it, but they didn't give me a date. Of course, they didn't stay in touch. After two weeks of radio silence, I decided they probably weren't going to be able to get it in, so I looked elsewhere. As luck would have it, I found the perfect car about three hours away from me. I had a friend drive down with me and we picked up my new car.

As luck would have it, on my way home in my new car, the salesperson from the first dealership called:

"I found the car that you're looking for, and I can have it here next week."

I said, "Wow, I wish I'd known that sooner. I'm driving my new car right now. I just bought it today, and I'm on my way home."

Obviously annoyed and rejected, he sighed. "Why did you look for one somewhere else when I already told you I could get it in?"

"I'm really sorry, but I have not heard from you for two weeks. I had no idea if you were still looking or how long it might take. I saw what I wanted, so I bought it."

He could not get it through his head that it was his failure to follow up along the way that cost him the sale. During the previous two weeks, I didn't get a single email text or phone call from him to let me know that he was still actively looking. If he had communicated to me that he was on the lookout for a car for me, I probably wouldn't have gone looking on my own. Because that was not communicated to me, my mind created a problem that did not exist and went out and solved it. That's what humans do!

This happens every day in salerooms and businesses across the world. Lack of communication leads to missed opportunities, disappointments, and hard feelings. It unravels months of hard work.
Networking and relationship-building stop, and those valuable seeds you have planted are stifled in the ground never to grow into a harvest. It's like putting seeds in the soil and then neglecting to water them because "it should rain soon."

Never worry about over communicating as long as you're not being pushy and trying to sell a product. If you're just checking in to let your client know that you're working on something they have asked you to do, they will appreciate and value your time.

The number one rejection I get when I tell other salespeople that they need to stay in touch is "I don't have time to reach out to people proactively. Do you know how many prospects I have? I've told them that I'm working on it and that should be good enough. People don't like it when you call them all the time and bother them." These are all foolish perspectives and will lead to lost clientele.

These are the same salespeople that you will see leaving the industry in a year or two or complaining about the lack of loyalty from their clients. There is a huge difference between cold calling people to try to sell them something versus checking in just to say, "Here's where I am in the process of doing. Please let me know if you'd rather not be updated, but I just want to let you know what's going on."

Part of communicating isn't just answering the phone when people call or getting back to them when they leave a message.

We've talked about how, when you don't have all the answers and you delay calling someone back until you do have the answers, it creates a stress response. It adds to people's anxiety. The same thing holds true of emails and texts from clients or referral partners providing you information.

Maybe they don't even have a question, but they're just providing you information. It is imperative that you respond and acknowledge that you received the email. I can't tell you how many times I have worked with realtors, underwriters, and other professionals and decided, based on their responses, that I will never send them a referral.

If they can't follow up with me, I know they are not going to take care of the people I send their way.

Let me walk you through how this goes. First, they request documents from me. So, I gather up those documents or provide whatever information they need and send them. Then there is zero response. It's like I fell into a black hole. I don't even know if they received it or not. This happens across all industries and professions. As an animal lover with lots of livestock, I can tell you that the veterinary industry is not much different. A doctor or staff member may perform a test and then never provide you with the results. Or you send them information on your animal, and there is no response to say it was received. On my end, I have no idea if it was received or not. And I can feel my stress response kicking in.

- Did they get it or not?
- Should I call them and make sure?
- If I call them, am I going to be bothered or will they be annoyed that I bothered them?

The second thing it does is freaking annoys me! I put time and effort into finding the information or getting something done they said they needed. And they respond with silence — no confirmation or thanks.

I love to stay in communication with my client. It portrays me as the professional I am. And, eventually, I get to contact them with good news:

"Hey, good news. Your client is fully approved. Congratulations, you are good to close this file on the 31st of October. It was a pleasure working with you. Thanks for your time."

Surprisingly, sometimes when I send such good news to a real estate agent, I get nothing back in reply. I'll be honest — it's kind of a letdown and rubs me the wrong way. It makes me feel like my time is not valuable if they can't even be bothered to acknowledge my efforts or the fact that they've received this great information. They don't acknowledge that I've been working on something that I know is time sensitive because they <u>told</u> me it's time sensitive.

They've told me it's important, and they need an answer ASAP. I work as hard as I can to get it done. I deliver the good news. And then... crickets! Nothing! No response or acknowledgement. It's baffling.

The third thing that starts to happen is I start to wonder if it was even that important or if they were not getting the message at all. Perhaps there was a communication error or a receptionist took the message and didn't pass it on. Now, I have to take the additional step to resend it or call to confirm. It also means I will be much less motivated to work as hard for them in the future.

I followed up:

"Hey, I was just making sure you got my message. This mortgage is good to go."

Occasionally they say, "No, I didn't get the message. I'm so glad you reached out to me."

When I get that response, I give myself a pat on the back for following up. I saved our communication process from breaking down. But sometimes, I get a different answer:

"Yeah, I got that. Sorry, I was busy."

Whaaat?!!! When people do that, I make a mental note in my mind to never send them a referral. I will work with them if they ask me to work with them, but I will never send them a client referral because I don't ever want my clients to feel like they're not even worthy of a quick note of thanks or acknowledgement. My clients are worth the two seconds it takes to acknowledge an email or text.

On the flip side of this, I go out of my way to refer to the partners that go the extra mile. I know that I can trust them to respond in a timely manner, confirm when information is received, ask for clarification if they are unsure, and show gratitude along the way. I send them as much business as I can knowing that they will never embarrass me by irritating a customer with a lack of communication.

One of my absolute favourite people to refer to came from that kind of mutually responsive communication. I loved the vibe I got from her. It wasn't just that she communicated.

She seemed to really take the time to be engaging. Every time I sent her something, she sent me a quick thumbs up or a "Got it! Thanks!" When I had a question, I knew I could expect an answer quickly. I found myself referring clients to her and regularly getting referrals from her. One day I remarked:

"We sure do a lot of business together lately."

Her response was, "I just love the communication, I am so spoiled by it. I don't ever want to work with anyone else."

I felt the same way about her.

She understood what many business owners seem to have forgotten. You are never too busy to give great customer service.

When my clients send me documents, when they do what I've asked them to do, when they get back to me, when my referral partners say, "Hey, I got this done for you, or here's the information you asked for," it doesn't matter how busy I am. It doesn't matter how many things I have on the go. I hit the reply button and say, "thank you" right away. Even a thumbs up is good if they are someone I have that kind of a close relationship with.

I might not have time for a long email, but I at least acknowledge that I received it. If I don't, I look like I'm too busy to be bothered with them. I look ungrateful. I look like I don't value their business or think that I have enough clients to afford to lose one or two.

This is especially true if we have just essentially been on a marathon together. If we have been trying to solve a difficult problem or collaborate, and I am confirming that we got it done, that's a time to celebrate and to say, "Thank you! I could not have done this without you."

Think of a time when you accomplished something great. Maybe you landed a new job, solved a big problem, or completed a huge assignment. You are stoked and rush to share it with your friend, roommate or teammates.

Then you are deflated when, instead of "That's fantastic! Way to go!" or "Yes! Right on!" they burst your bubble of joy with a criticism or tell you they are too busy to talk right now. How did that make you feel?

Did you feel rejected, disappointed, discouraged? That's how your referral partners and team mates and clients feel when you don't take the time to celebrate and acknowledge their successes. You will create a feeling of comradery, create a feeling of teamwork when you take the time to shout, "Yay!! We did this right!"

I will always remember getting ready to write my broker exam; I was so nervous. I reached out to the person who inspired me to do it in the first place, a broker named Catherine Knight. She was incredibly busy, but she still took the time to send me a quick one-liner.

She said, "You will kill it!" I saved that response because it gave me the confidence I needed in the moment, and it made me feel important and valued. Make people feel that way and your business will grow beyond your wildest expectations.

But, you may ask, what about those challenging clients where communication is strained, or something has gone sideways? Let's have a look at that in the next chapter.

Notes

CHAPTER 13 – FIRE-BREATHING DRAGONS

*"If you are patient in a moment of
anger, you will escape a hundred
days of sorrow."*
~ *Chinese Proverb*

"Just do your job. Why do you keep asking me for all this crap? I've never missed a payment in my life. My credit is great. Just get me a mortgage already and stop making it so difficult!"

These were the words spoken to me by a woman who turned out to be my worst nightmare. She was angry. She was rude. She was hostile. She was belligerent. She was uncooperative. In short, she was the worst client ever.

I would ask her for specific documents. She would send me something completely different. I would go back to her and say, "Hey, this isn't exactly what I asked for." She would completely have an over-the-top freaked out reaction. On top of that, every day she would call for an update and ask, "Why isn't this done yet? What's taking so long." It got to the point that every time I saw her number come up on my phone, my stomach would start to twist, and I just wanted to run away and hide. It was keeping me up at night with worry and was affecting my productivity during the day. In order to do my job, I needed certain documents from her and I needed accurate information that she would not provide and was angry when asked.

Finally, I realized that I was going to need to fire her. For my own sanity, I needed to let her go. It took me an entire day to muster my courage, but finally I just decided to do it. I decided to rip off the band aid and get that horrible conversation over with.

I had already tried in a nice way; I had suggested that her own bank could probably do the mortgage faster than I could, and I had said that other brokers who had more experience with bruised credit could probably do a better job. She never wanted to hear that though. She just said "I asked you to work on it, not someone else. Just get it done already."

The day came to part company with her. I took a big breath, pushed away all my anxiety, and I dialed the number. I kept hoping for voicemail but, alas, she picked up the phone and before I could change my mind.

"Hey," I said. "I just need to let you know… I'm not going to be able to work on your file anymore. It's not working out for me. I'm not able to get the information from you that I'm asking for, and without those documents it's a hard stop for lenders. This is not something I can fix or that I have any control over. I have a lot of other clients who need my help. I need to focus on the ones who are willing to provide me the information I need to get them an approval. This is taking up a lot of my time and I didn't become self-employed to have someone yell at me and be rude to me. So, you tell me where you want to go. I will send your file there. I will send all your information. I will call them and make sure they have all your information. You don't need to do anything. I will make sure it's a seamless transition to a new person. Just let me know where you want it to go."

Total silence on the end of the phone.

"Hello?"

And then I heard sniffing, sobbing, and crying. I felt like crap and thought I must have called her in the middle of some family emergency.

"Are you okay? Did I call it a bad time?"

"I'm sorry," she cried. "I know I'm acting like a crazy person, but you are my last hope. My landlord is selling my house. I have three kids. There are no rentals in the valley. I have nowhere to go. If I don't get this mortgage, I think I'm going to be homeless. Three other mortgage brokers have already turned me down and you were my last hope. And now you don't want to work with me either. What am I going to do?"

I immediately thought, "Oh boy, did I ever get this wrong." I thought she was angry. She was not angry. **She was scared**. When we are scared, this thing happens in our brain. We go back thousands of years in our development from our reptile brain. Normally, when we perceive a physical threat, our body goes into fight or flight mode. We need that response so we can punch that grizzly bear in the nose if we have to.

It's there in case we have to run away or pick up a spear or whatever. The point is we have the courage, muscle strength, pupil dilation, and blood flow necessary to take an action. Our bodies supply us with ample adrenaline to make us strong and fast and brave.

We don't think about consequences; we just think about overcoming the threat as quickly as possible.

But what about when a threat isn't physical? What happens when we can't pick up a weapon and defend ourselves? Particularly in the modern world that is relatively safe, most of our threats are emotional and/or psychological. In that case, adrenaline is not being used for some demanding physical activity. But it is still there and available in the body. So, it turns to rage, and we try to express it verbally. We may try to control our threatening situation by verbally attacking or controlling the people and the situation or by running away.

But this poor woman was trapped. She could not run away from her tragic housing situation. So, she was fighting with words. She was using the only weapons she had: her words and her voice through the phone and emails.

We abhor feeling powerless. It is one of the most uncomfortable feelings any person can have. And when one of our basic needs — like housing — is not being met, it can be terrifying.

At that moment I remembered something that a colleague, Scott Peckford, said on his podcast, *I Love Mortgage Brokering*:

> *"When you run into these situations, you need to remember, you did not create the situation. You're like the paramedic who shows up at an emergency; you weren't the drunk driver. You didn't cause a heart attack; you are just there to help."*

I asked Scott about this and it turns out before he was a mortgage broker, he was a paramedic, and that was the advice his mentor had given to him. It is still sound advice in any industry.

Most times, you did not create the problem, you are just there to help.

So, I took a breath and I said, "Hey, listen, I'm just here to help. I want you to get into a house. I do not want you to be homeless. I am losing sleep over this, but I can't help you unless you're willing to work with me. Can you get me the pay stub and the T-4s that I've been asking for?"

"No," she said quietly.

"No? Ok? You can't or you won't?"

"Well, I have them, but I haven't been working full time. They only show part-time hours. So, there's no point even sending them to you."

I thought for a moment before responding. "You told me that you always pay your bills on time and your credit is perfect. So how are you paying your bills?"

"Well, I get the child tax credit."

I thought, okay, now we are getting somewhere. "How much is your child tax credit?"

"It's about $1800 a month," she said starting to sound a bit hopeful. "I have three kids. Oh, and I get child support too." She seemed happy that this was information she could provide.

"Awesome. Can you send me proof of that?"

Her tone was changing to empowerment and excitement, "Yes!"

"Beautiful. I am going to need those documents, proof of your kids ages, and a separation agreement showing the child support. Do you have any other income?"

She paused for a moment. "Well, yeah, I just actually started a new full-time job. I make even more than I did at my old job. But I was told that lenders won't take your income if you're on probation, so I didn't want to tell you about that."

Well, hello? Why did I not have this information sooner? But I remained patient.

"Is it in the same line of work that you've done before?"

"Yes."

This was just getting better by the minute. I could smell the approval!

"There are exceptions to that rule. And if there's a good reason, I can get that exception approved. Can you get a job letter and a pay stub from your new job and two years of T-4s from your old one to show that you've been in the same line of work?"

Totally on board now, she practically yelled, "Yes I can!"

"Great!" Then my tone turned quite serious.
"I'm going to need one other thing from you. And this is going to be a hard one, but if you can get me this, I think we can get this file done."

"OK, what is it?"

I answered with a totally deadpan tone, "Can you bring me your firstborn child?"

There was an awkward silence until she realized I was joking and then we both cracked up as we began to move forward in a new spirit of cooperation. With the new information and documents, I was able to get her approved for a mortgage at a great rate with good terms. She was able to buy a house for her little family and I have since helped her with a second purchase of a revenue property.

That was one of the most difficult, but also one of the most satisfying, files of my career. I still remember exactly where I was and how I felt when that approval came in. It was a high that lasted all day and giving her the good news was the highlight of my month.

After the file was all done, she texted me to say, "I think I am going through withdrawal. I'm used to talking to you every day, and I have not talked to you for at least a week. It feels so weird."

The lesson here is that sometimes anger is just a cover for something else and if you can dig deep and get to the bottom of it, you may be able to forge a new relationship and find solutions you did not even think were possible. You must ask the right questions and be willing to stand your ground with kindness to get to the root of the fear and address it.

I'm going to give you 2 tips to help you with this:

— **First, change the way you think about that angry client.**

I want you to think of a little scared kitten that's been injured and abandoned and that you have just found it in a ditch. It's scared and hissing and spitting. You suspect that it might try to kill you. But you don't react with anger because you know it's just a scared kitten.

Angry clients are the same way; at the core of their anger and rudeness is fear. They are just scared kittens, and the way to get through to them is to resolve the cause of the fear and build trust. If you respond with anger or rudeness, you will amplify the situation. If you validate their feelings and find out why they are afraid, you will build a relationship.

That scared kitten is not really angry. It's hungry, thirsty, lost, and alone. So, you take it home, dry it off, and treat its wounds. You win its trust by showing it that you are there to help. Before long, it has gone from hissing and spitting to purring and trusting. You may find you end up with a dream client and a long-term deep relationship formed in the trust of helping them overcome an obstacle.

— Second, empathize

You don't know the cause of someone's fear unless you ask questions. If you don't get to the root of the problem, you can't address it. You can say things like: "I can see you are worried, and I want to help, but I need to know what the issue is." Often clients will give you clues to their fear in the words they use while angry. For example, at a veterinary hospital, a client will call at 9pm with a sick animal and, when told that the doctors have gone back home and there will be an emergency fee for them to leave their family and come back into work, the client flies into a rage. "All you people care about is money. You don't care about animals. What a scam!"

At first glance this client seems like a real ass hat, right? I mean the doctor has already worked 12 hours straight, she's got kids and family like everyone else, and now she must pack up and come back in. Any reasonable person would say she deserves to be paid for her time. The staff loves animals, and they don't want to see one suffer, but they are not authorized to waive the fees.

What the staff of the animal hospital needs to remember is that this client is in fight or flight mode right now. If the staff isn't careful, they will also be triggered and get drawn into the same flight/flight mode from the verbal abuse they are taking from the client.

That will result in an angry customer who might pay for this emergency but may never visit the vet's office again.

If they can first remember the wet kitten analogy and second, empathise and ask questions instead of being reactive and hurt, they can start to find a path forward.

One receptionist was being yelled at because "all veterinarians are greedy bastards." Rather than respond with anger, she might have said, "Oh my gosh, I have a dog too, and I understand how upsetting it is when pets are sick. I wonder if maybe we could start by assessing if this is a true emergency or if there is something you could do to make your pet more comfortable until morning. Would you like to speak to a technician so she can get more information?" Which brings us to our third point:

— Third, ask questions

Find out more information. Is this a true emergency and is it the emergency fee that has triggered all of the rage? If so, that is your first clue that this is really about scarcity — usually economic scarcity — and the helplessness it brings at being unable to financially care for a pet.

This may not be in the receptionist's control to fix, but it can help them communicate better. Using the kitten analogy, the receptionist can remain calm and helpful in the knowledge that it was not personal and that it was about helplessness. That mindset makes it easier to take those calls, to be compassionate, and not to take the insults home. Then she can think clearly to help the client, like letting them know about veterinary financing options which would allow them to spread out the cost of care to better fit their budget.

If you can remember in the heat of the moment, first think of difficult people as a scared child or a scared animal who feels unsafe. Realize they are just lashing out to protect themselves and you are just there to help.

Remind yourself that you didn't create this problem. If you can let go of the responsibility for creating the problem, you can feel calmer.

Second, empathize, put yourself in their shoes, relate to them, and be kind. And three, you must ask the questions. When you ask the questions, you find out the reasons. When you find out the reasons, you can address the fear and move forward to find solutions.

The next time you come across that angry, raging client, I want you to remember, they're afraid. Remember that you're there to help, be empathetic, ask the questions and move forward in a spirit of cooperation.

Notes

CHAPTER 14 - OWN YOUR MISTAKES

"Failure is a great teacher, and I think when you make mistakes and you recover from them and you treat them as valuable learning experiences, then you've got something to share."
~ Steve Harvey

Speaking of angry clients, sometimes despite our best efforts, we screw up. And no matter how good you are at your job, let me assure you, mistakes will happen. When they do happen, it's how we handle them that shows people who we really are and determines how the client will react also.

Our human pride tells us to find someone or something else to blame. It's part of that reptile fight or flight response. It's one of those things from evolutionary biology that does not serve us anymore. Back in the caveman days, if you screwed up and put the tribe in danger, you might be executed for your mistake. It was important to find a scapegoat to keep yourself safe. Today, failing to take responsibility or blaming someone else just makes you look weak and incapable of learning from your mistakes or taking ownership of them.

Let's look at an example. I had been working on a particular file for months. I finally got it done. Two days before it was supposed to be funded, I got a call from my client. He said, "I just heard from the lawyer's office. They're not going to be able to complete this transaction on time. What is going on?"

Let me tell you, this is not a call that anybody wants to get in my position. I sprang into action to deal with the monumental task of getting this file through to the finish line. It was very time sensitive. There was a domino effect on other properties and sales.

Not only did this person need the sale to close, but several other people's transactions also were depending on the closing date.

This could quickly turn into a nightmare for myself, my clients, the other realtor, their client, and the other buyers and sellers on the other end of the transaction. It was like this little string that, if you pull on it, the entire spool will unravel.

The first thing I did was take a breath. That may seem like a nonsensical thing to do, but it is the right first step in any crisis. Taking a breath does about a dozen things for your situation. But the most important thing is that it gives you a moment to sit with the problem to all of its component parts to settle in your mind. It fills your blood with oxygen which has a dramatic effect on your mental clarity, creativity, and decision-making ability. Lastly, it gives your brain a chance to process solutions.

I picked up the phone and called the lawyer's office and spoke to the Conveyancer:

"Hey, I hear that you may have difficulty closing this on time. Can you help me understand what happened? I sent you all the details about a month ago. I gave you the extra documents you requested. And, when I checked in last week, I asked if you'd be able to complete on time. I understood that you would. Now it's supposed to close in two days and the client tells me that you haven't even started, and you are not going to be able to complete on time."

There was a pause at the other end of the line while the Conveyancer looked up the details. "Oh, that file. Yeah, we're not going to be able to get that done in two days. That's not enough time."

Gently, but firmly I again reiterated, "It is not 2 days. It's been a month, and I've been checking in regularly. I was promised that it would get done on time. I'm just wondering, what happened between a month ago and now?"

I was expecting to hear "Oh my gosh, I'm so sorry. We made a mistake. We dropped the ball. Let's see what we can figure out." Instead, her tone changed. It became hostile. It became defensive. It became argumentative.

"Well, this isn't my fault. We're running busy right now. You should have been calling every day to check on this. If you had called me two days ago, I would have told you this couldn't be done. We are down a staff member; I have been swamped with files. I asked someone else to do it, and they didn't. It's not my fault. The market is busy, so you can't expect me to drop everything and just push this through now. The clients are just going to have to deal with the new date."

Again, I took another deep breath because I knew that getting angry in this situation was going to make her defensiveness worse. Just like we talked about in a previous chapter, she was now responding from a place of fear that was translating as anger.
She had just realized the huge mistake she had made. She had been called on the carpet for dropping the ball. And she was now projecting anger onto me as a defense mechanism to get herself out of what she perceived to be a mess that she knew she made, but didn't want to take responsibility for.

I answered politely. "I know it's a really busy time right now. I know everyone is swamped. But I did ask you last week, if you could do this. I made sure that you had everything that you needed. I asked if you needed anything else, what can I do to help you to get this done on time? The clients cannot change their date. There are a whole bunch of other sales that are linked to this sale, and they're all going to fall apart if this doesn't get done. How can I help you get this done? Let me know what I can do, who I can call, or what documents you need. But this has to get done."

Because I didn't blame her, even though she was completely at fault, her defenses came down just a little bit.

"Well, let me see what I can do." And she hung up the phone.

I ended up calling the actual lawyer and explained the problem to him without placing blame on anyone. I also conveyed the urgency to him and why it needed to get done on time. As a result, they were able to come through, and we were able to get it completed. I will say this, I never used that law firm again for anything.
Even though they got it done, even though they came through in the end, they severed any future relationship. I will never work with someone who is not willing to accept responsibility or with someone who makes their mistake my problem.

I know I can't work with people whose first impulse is to immediately respond with fear and blame instead of taking ownership. The reality is that most people will never return for repeat business once they have experienced that.

The rookie mistake is to think that shifting blame away from your mistake will salvage a damaged relationship and make you look better in the eyes of the client. Really though, the exact opposite is true. I have more confidence, more trust in someone that is willing to say, "Oh, my goodness. I screwed up. I'm sorry. How can I fix this?" than I do when someone says, "This wasn't my fault." Taking responsibility speaks to their integrity. It speaks to honesty. It speaks to willingness to own your problems and fix them.

The minute someone plays that blame-shifting game with me, the minute they try to explain to me why it's not their fault, I lose all respect for them. I don't want to work with them ever again. And that's what happens to you when you make a mistake and you try to deflect the blame away from yourself. It's not professional or honest to make it your client's fault or the company's fault or the manufacturer's fault or anyone else's fault.
When you shift the blame away from the real culprit, you look dishonest, like someone who lacks integrity.

Let me tell you about a different scenario. I had another file that I had sent to a different lawyer. This was a file that I was not directly getting paid a commission on.

The way that I got paid was to charge the client a fee for my services. To make sure that happened, I sent documents to the lawyer directing them to collect the fee from the clients when the funds were given to them from the mortgage.

It's basically a letter that the client signed instructing the lawyer to collect my fee and send it to me. And it was a significant amount, enough to pay most of my mortgage that month. Just to be thorough, I had called a lawyer as well, as I always do to follow up.

"I just wanted to let you know, there's a letter of transmittal in with the documents and you are going to need to collect my fee from the proceeds of the mortgage and send it to me when it completes."

She said, "Yeah, no problem. I saw that, I've made a note of it, and I'll make sure it happens."

I thought, great, this is dealt with. I didn't give it another thought. Two weeks after that file closed, I realized that I hadn't yet received that fee yet. There was no deposit to my bank account. No check had arrived. So, I called up the lawyer.

"Hi! I'm just curious, I'm wondering if maybe there's been a delay, but that file closed a couple of weeks ago and I've never received payment."

"Well, what do you mean? It's all done, it's closed."

"Don't you remember that we talked about that letter of transmittal, and you were supposed to collect the $2,000 for me and send it to me."

Suddenly there was a silence on the other end of the line while she processed the reality that this hadn't been done. Here's the difference though, between this file and the last file. Instead of placing blame, instead of making it my fault somehow instead of making excuses and telling me how busy she was, she owned it. She didn't have to; she could have blamed a busy market or a careless worker in her office.

I know for a fact that she was screaming busy because she was answering my emails after midnight and also at seven o'clock in the morning. So, she was putting in sixteen to eighteen hours per day.

And it would have been easy for her to say that she was so busy it slipped her mind or that I was unrealistic to expect her to remember everything. But she didn't do any of those things. She didn't pass the buck or shift the blame.

"Oh my gosh, I am so sorry. I completely missed that. This is my fault. Let me fix it. I will call the client right now. I will explain to them it was my mistake and I will get her to bring those funds back in."

"Wow," I said. "Are you sure? That's going to be a very difficult conversation. I mean, it's already closed. They might've already spent that money."

She said, "Don't worry about it. It's not your problem. It's my problem. It's going to suck to have that conversation. If I must, I will write you the check out of my own account. But this is not your fault. It's my fault. And I'm going to fix it. I'll get back to you as soon as it's resolved."

Two days later, she called me.

"The client is coming back tomorrow and is bringing a bank draft for your $2,000 commission. I will have it sent to you. I explained to the client that this was not your fault, that it was an oversight, and it was our fault. I hope that you will trust us in the future. I want you to know that I've put a few safeguards in place to make sure this doesn't happen again. We have created a closing checklist to make sure that this doesn't happen in the future."

What was different between that transaction and the woman in the previous transaction. First, she owned her mistake... immediately! She said, "I made a mistake," and then promised that she was going to fix it. Upon hearing those words, my stress subsided. I no longer had to worry that I was going to have to be the one to call up this client and tell her that she still owed me $2,000. That would have tainted my relationship with the client and would have affected my future referrals. Besides, I just really didn't want to have to do that."

I was prepared to say it was my mistake even though it wasn't. I would have fallen on that sword because that would have been preferable to blaming the lawyer's office. I would have taken all of the blame.

But this lawyer ensured that I didn't have to do that by taking responsibility for herself. Secondly, she kept her word and fixed the problem. She made sure I got paid.

She did the right thing. But the magic of her integrity was in the final step. She assured me that she had explained everything to my client, preserving my relationship with her and then worked to ensure that she learned something from her mistake. Her heartfelt sorry was followed by a promise that I would be able to trust her in the future.

You know what? I will trust her 100% of the time in the future. Yes, she made a big mistake, but the way she handled it absolutely 100% confirmed to me that that is someone I want to work with going forward. In fact, if I had a choice, I would send every client to that person in the future, because I know she's trustworthy. I know she will honor her word. And I know that if she makes a mistake, she will fix it. And that's what you need to do. Also, when you make a mistake, you need to own it. You need to fix it. That will build trust and create relationships that last a lifetime.

The question is not if you will make a mistake. It's when. We are human; mistakes will happen. When they do you can choose to react in a way that deepens trust, shows integrity, and builds a stronger relationship. On the other hand, you can create fear, resentment and distrust.

In the next chapter, we will cover the companion to this topic: keeping your word.

Notes

CHAPTER 15 – KEEPING YOUR WORD

*"The value of your work is not in
the dollar. It is in your word."*
~ Jennifer Ho-Dougatz

Imagine two different scenarios. In the first scenario, you realized that your dishwasher is busted. You call up your local repair shop and tell the repairman the problem. But he says he's busy today. He offers to come out to your house tomorrow but warns that he is not sure what time because he has a busy day. The best he can promise is that he will be there after lunch sometime.

You leave work early, go home, clear the stuff out from under the sink, and then you wait for him to show up. At 2p, there is no sign of him. But since he did say after lunch, you figure that could be anytime before about 3ish. You wait and you wait. 5pm comes and goes with no sign of him. You try calling but just get voicemail.

You are frustrated that you have taken time off from work. Besides, you have all the stuff from under your sink piled up. An hour later, you are still waiting. No repair guy. The afternoon ends. At 6pm, you call, but the call rolls to voicemail.

The next day he calls back and says, "Yeah, sorry. I got busy, and I didn't have time to make it over there. How about tomorrow?" Are you going to believe him and use his services? Or are you going to call someone else who is more reliable? Regardless of what you decide to do, you will never trust his word again. He has just shown you that his word is worth nothing.

If you let him work on your appliance, and he tells you he has to order a part. When he says it should only take a day, will you believe him? No, you will have doubts, and you surely won't feel comfortable taking off another day to meet him at your house.

As humans we are programmed by evolution to figure out very quickly who can be trusted and who cannot. People who don't keep their word are not to be trusted. The repair guy likely doesn't even realize the harm he has done. He's thinking he just got busy and ran out of time. He may think that this is the way it is with all repairmen, and you just have to live with it. But when he told you he would be there and wasn't, that is not something you will forget. In the future, if you have a choice between using him or using someone reliable, you will choose the reliable guy. If you are asked to leave a review it probably won't be great.

The act of not keeping your word will have a ripple effect on other transactions, on reviews, and on the referrals that people send. Your repair guy won't go bankrupt today from it, but business is about the long game. And he just lost a major round. Over the course of a decade, it will reduce his business. He may be in a business that's highly in demand right now. He may be able to afford to make some people angry. But overtime, he will pay the price when his lack of integrity affects his relationships with suppliers, partners, colleagues, and most importantly, customers.

On the other hand, what about that person who always keeps their word? You know the one who makes a promise you can set your watch by. If they owe you money it will be repaid and repaid in full. If they promise they will be somewhere, they show up early. If they offer to do something, they go above and beyond. Those are the kind of people who cultivate relationships without even trying. People are naturally drawn to them simply because they keep their word and are reliable. They rise high and fast in organizations.

Let's look at a different example. Sarah started out as a brand-new business development manager with no experience. She was promoted into the role from another part of the company because clients started asking for her by name and management noticed this and decided to give her a shot. In her first year, she did more production than both of the long-term business development managers did.

Clients from outside her territory started to ask to work with her. Management was thrilled but puzzled at her meteoric rise.

So, they asked clients what was so special about her? After all, she had no sales experience and didn't have that much product knowledge. They had to figure out what her secret sauce was that made everyone want to work with her.

Do you know what the answer was? Person after person reported that she was reliable, she called people back when she said she would, and was always pleasant. If she didn't know the answer, she promised to find out and then did. If her clients ran into a problem, she said, "I will take care of this" and then she actually did.

The other BDMs promise a lot but they never delivered. If there was a problem, they said they will fix it, but they didn't, and then they stopped answering their phones when pushed to come through. They often blamed others claiming that the problem was outside of their control.

Doing what you say you are going to do is more than just being a good person. It builds trust and makes your clients feel valued and safe in your hands. They feel like they are working with someone of integrity who cares about them.

I remember years ago having the opportunity to join a certain company. They kept saying they were busy and wanted to talk about it another day. Tomorrow, tomorrow, tomorrow was their constant battle cry. But tomorrow never came. I would give them a little nudge and again, I'd hear, "I'll call you tomorrow." Still no call. In the course of being stood up so many times, I realized this was not a company I wanted to go into partnership with. If they could not keep their word on something as simple as a phone call, what else would they not keep their word about? I ended up joining another firm.

The firm I rejected finally did call and asked me about partnering again. When I told them I had gone elsewhere, they could not believe it. They said, "But you were going to join my company! I was ready to make you a great offer. Why didn't you tell me you were looking at other options?"

The truth is that up until they reneged on their promise to call me three times in a row, I was not looking at other options.

But I was grateful to find out what they were about early on. They told me this was not the first time someone had jumped ship at the last minute and that they could not understand how so many people changed their mind at the last minute. I suspect I was not the only one who didn't appreciate being stood up and the lack of reliability.

If you say you are going to do something, you darn well better do it. If something changes and you can't honor your commitment, then pick up the phone and explain why with a plan to reschedule. But don't just blow it off. If you are the least bit unsure, just don't promise. Never make a promise you don't intend to or cannot keep. Underpromise and overdeliver (we'll cover this in more detail in a moment). Set expectations honestly so that you can knock it out of the park when you are able to give more than you promised you would.

Once you lose credibility, you will never get it back. The best way to keep your credibility is to never lose it in the first place. Sometimes despite our best efforts, we literally forget an appointment, or a genuine emergency arises. When that happens, we need to sincerely and genuinely apologize and then show through actions that it is not the norm.

Let's say you are a contractor when you promise someone you will have their home finished by July 15. They plan the rest of their life around that date. They make plans to move and take the week off work. They sell their other home expecting to be in their remodeled home by the agreed upon date. Now imagine July 15 rolls around and you see that you are not going to be done. You've just completely turned the customer's life upside down.

 At that point, nobody cares what your reasons are. They don't care if the delays were unexpected or if weather factored in. All they care about is that you said you do something and you didn't get it done. This goes for pricing also. If you promise something will cost a certain amount of money and then you raise the price afterwards you look dishonest.

But how do you account for the unexpected then? How do you factor in the sudden supplier price increase or the unexpected delays that invariably happen?

There are a few things you can do.

The first is to go back and look at the chapter on communication. Remember that silence is deadly; so are delays in transmitting changes to agreed terms. The minute you know that you are facing a potential issue and something will be different than discussed, you need to be on the phone with your client and make them aware. You don't have to be all doom and gloom and create anxiety; you can show them that you are proactively dealing with it while also ensuring it does not come as a surprise at the last minute. Some people actually spring changes in price or delivery on their customers at the last minute and then are shocked at their angry reaction.

Let's look at the builder example. The builder may be part way through building a home for someone to whom he has already given them a quote when he gets a notification that the cost of drywall just went up.

He should immediately start looking at alternative options and present them. He should NOT wait to have that conversation but should get on the phone immediately and say, "Look, I have just received notice that the cost of drywall has increased. This is out of my control, but it is going to add xx dollars to your final cost. We have a couple of options here. The first option is that we can try and buy it in advance of when we need it at current pricing and store it. The downside is that the bank is only advancing your funds in stages, so it will leave you short on money for framing. If you have any extra savings or credit you have access to in the short term, this would save you money in the long term."

"The second option is that it's not too late to scale back the square footage a bit and make the garage a single instead of a double. That would be enough to make up the difference.

"The third option is you can go back to the bank and let them know about the change and see if you can get approved for more funds."

This method gives the customer solutions to consider and allows you to get in front of the problem. This allows you to keep your word as best you can.

You may not be able to deliver everything exactly as quoted, but you have given a valid reason why and options well in advance so there is no surprise extra bill at the end.

In addition to communicating changes *as soon as you know about them* and working with your client on a solution, you can set expectations early on by under promising and over delivering. What does this mean? This means you build a buffer into your pricing or your timeframe that allows for possible issues along the way.

I remember years ago working with a veterinarian who was very busy and always running behind. He never knew how long each appointment was going to take, so he was careful with his words. One day I overheard him training a new vet student, and the new guy was on the phone to a client. Just as the vet student was just hanging up, he said, "OK I'll see you in 15 minutes."

The older vet who was training him turned to him and said, "Never say that on a house call. Never give an exact time. Say, 'I'll get there as soon as I can.'" He added, "You have no idea if you can keep that promise. An emergency could walk in the door, or this dog you are vaccinating now could have a reaction, and you might have to stay longer. Never, never promise to be at a house call at a certain time. It sets an expectation. Then, if you can't keep it, you look like a jerk."

He was right if you truly cannot control the outcome then don't promise it.

How would this look for a real estate transaction?

If a client asks how long it will take to get their mortgage funded and money in the bank, you might be tempted to give them a very short timeline so they don't walk away. But if you can't definitely complete on time, what did that promise cost your business?
You effectively turned yourself into a hunter instead of a farmer. You will get their business this one time because now they are halfway into it and it's too late to walk. But you won't get that repeat business or referrals.

A better thing to do might be to give them the worst-case scenario so they are prepared for it, and then let them know you will do your absolute best to do it faster. For example, if someone is refinancing their home and they are in a hurry to get funded, they may ask how long it takes.

The temptation is to say, "I can definitely do this in a few days" because you know that's what they want to hear, but it's not a truthful answer in every case. A better thing might be to say, "I will make this a priority.

If everything goes perfectly and I have all your documents up front, I may be able to call in a few favours and get it rushed. Hopefully, I can get this done by the end of the week. But I don't have a crystal ball though and any little hiccup along the way could delay this. The appraisal could take longer, or someone could be on holidays. The worst-case scenario is likely two weeks, but I will do my best to get it done faster."

That sets the expectation that there could be delays but you will be on their side doing your best. If it gets done quickly, you look like a rockstar; if it is delayed at least, they know ahead of time it could happen. If the worst-case scenario is just totally unacceptable to them, it gives them a chance to say so. At that point, you should let them go and wish them well, or say you will make some calls and get back to them. But at least you are not making fake promises. Promising and not delivering is worse than having them walking away.

Remember it doesn't matter how big or small a transaction is, your ability to keep your word means the difference between planting seeds that grow or finding a quick meal and never having that resource available to you again.

Return phone calls when you say you will, honor your pricing, pay your bills, keep your promises. These are the kinds of actions that grow, attract, and keep clients year after year.

In the next chapter we will talk about another kind of honesty and how it will impact your relationships.

Notes

CHAPTER 16 - LIFE IS NOT FICTION – DON'T MAKE THINGS UP

"I'm not upset that you lied to me.
I'm upset that from now on, I can't
believe you."
~ Friedrich Nietzsche

When I first decided to become a mortgage broker, I had no idea what I was doing. I had no clue how much networking and relationship building and sales it involved, and I thought it would be just entering numbers into a system, pushing a button and voila you get an approval, the client thinks you are amazing and repeat.

The reality was that I felt completely lost, I knew nothing, I felt like I was in kindergarten all over again learning to read and write. There were so many terms to learn. Even the simplest things seemed overwhelming.

The first time I took an application, I had no idea what I was doing, but I had to act as if I did. I took all their information and asked questions. I listened and nodded every time they asked me a question. I didn't know the answer to most of their questions. But I was at least able to say, "Let me check on that. The rules in this industry change all the time and I don't want to give you a wrong answer."

That was not untrue as the rules do change constantly, and I didn't want to give a wrong answer, But the reality was I simply did not know the answers. I could not tell my client that I didn't know. They would have lost confidence in me, and I would look like I didn't know what I was doing. No one would have trusted me with their home purchase if I gave out the wrong information and looked like an idiot later when the truth turned out to be something different.

It turns out this was a good strategy because, years later, my first client came back to me (and did many times after that). I felt comfortable finally confessing to him that he was my first file. He was so surprised. He said, "I felt like I was dealing with a very experienced professional. I felt totally safe and well cared for like you knew what you were doing. You never gave me bad advice, and you had all the correct answers."

I was happy to hear that I looked like a professional because I acted like one and I had all the right answers because I never made stuff up.

In an earlier chapter, we covered what it means to *act as if*. But be careful. *Acting as if* it is acting. But it is not inventing things out of thin air. *Acting as if* it is a mindset. It is an air of confidence that exudes from you. But it should not come from fabricated or invented information.

Acting as if means that, regardless of how the new you feels, you need to act like someone who has been doing this for decades. You need to present yourself as a professional because that is what you are. You might not be an experienced professional. But you are still a professional. The answers you do know, you need to fully investigate and get back to the client. Once you research them, learn and memorize them so that, in the future, you can answer on the spot with knowledge and confidence.

Newcomers have a terrible time with this. When they don't know the answers, they stutter, rifle through papers, sweat, shift their bodies or their eyes. Everything about them screams, "Amateur." Keep your cool. The customer doesn't know if the answer to their question is complex and technical or if it is common knowledge. They don't know the answer either, which is why they asked you.

Don't worry about looking bad in jotting a question down and promising to get the answer to the customer soon. By the way, soon is within 24 hours. You should be on the phone or sending an email with the answers to all of their questions. Any longer and you look both incompetent and non-communicative.

Let's take Bob for instance, he sold me my first electric car, and he was a new sales guy. The most important feature for me as a purchaser was the hands-free texting capability as I always have clients texting me. I wanted to be able to auto-reply with my voice or send a preloaded reply. I asked him specifically if this was an option. He didn't know for sure but he didn't want to disappoint me as he could see it was an important feature. He said, "Yes, of course, it has all the latest hands-free technology."

He assumed that, since it was an electric car and had a lot of technology in it, that it would have that option as a standard feature. The truth is that he really didn't know. It was so easy for him to take a second and look over the features list to find the answer. But he fabricated. And I trusted him. Based on the information he gave me, I went ahead and ordered a new car.

I did the financing, sold my old car, and eagerly awaited the arrival of my new car. What was I most looking forward to? Obviously! The ability to either turn on an autoresponder to say I was driving or to respond with simple phrases like" I'm on my way" or "I'll get back to you."

With great excitement I drove down to the dealership, and the salesman met me to do the insurance paperwork and go over the features of my new car. I only really cared about one feature and that was the hands-free texting. I was so sick of constantly pulling over to the side of the road every time my phone dinged. I was in an industry where you have to respond quickly to texts and calls. I could not afford to wait to get to my destination to let people know I had received a text. I was so excited to have this problem removed from my life.

(This is also why its important to ask good questions and understand your clients' motivations but we will get to that in a later chapter.)

I didn't care about all the other features he was showing me. But he just kept going through them.

"Just show me how to text hands free," I insisted. "That's the reason I am getting the car."

His mouth seemed to go dry and he broke out in a cold sweat. "Oh, um. Yeah, um... the hands-free texting. I'm, um, not sure how exactly it works. But you can check the manual. I'm sure you can figure it out when you get home."

I was a bit deflated since I was not the type to read manuals. So, I pressed him. "Can you get someone that knows how to work it or grab the manual. This is really important to me, and I want to know how to use it before I leave here."

He said, "Oh, yeah. Ok, let me grab a service person."

The service person came back and tried to help.

"I don't know about this car but, in mine, you just hook up the Bluetooth and it works."

He helped me hook up my Bluetooth, but when I tried to reply to a text, the screen displayed the dreaded words: "that feature is not available." I was getting concerned and annoyed.

"It says that feature is not available. What does that mean? Does it need an update or something?"

They both started to look a bit concerned at this point.

"Well," the salesman said, "I guess maybe it doesn't work on iPhones — just with android."

"Well, I have an iPhone," I said, getting frustrated. "I just bought this car specifically for this feature."

He went to get his manager who confirmed that the feature did not work with my phone. He said it could probably be fixed with a new phone. Or I could wait a year or two for the manufacturer to offer an update to my kind of phone.

I nearly lost my mind at that point, but what could I do? I had done the financing, sold my old car, signed all the papers.

But the main thing I wanted in the car was not available because a new salesperson assumed, did not check for the right answer, and gave me incorrect advice. Long story short, the dealership ended up buying me a new phone that would work with the car. But it was not a fun learning curve for me or the salesperson. I was so angry; I think I told everyone I knew the dealership story for weeks. I never went back to that dealership and never sent that salesman a referral. The lesson here is act as if you know but don't make things up. Say "things change all the time, let me check."

Act like you are just verifying and find out for sure. It's important to act like you know what you are doing when you don't but not to the point of making stuff up. Even people who have been in an industry for decades still ask questions. They still say, "I'm not sure, but I'll find out.

Having someone experienced and knowledgeable to ask will change everything so find someone you trust and can rely on to go to for accurate answers to difficult questions. This leads me to my next chapter on Mentoring.

Notes

CHAPTER 17 - MENTORSHIP MATTERS

"A mentor is not someone who walks ahead of us and tells us how they did it. A mentor is someone who walks alongside us to guide us on what we can do.
~ Simon Sinek

A mentor/mentee relationship is one of the most amazing relationships you will ever experience. You should not only seek out a mentor, but you should also aspire to mentor others whenever you have the opportunity. It will grow your network, enrich your life, boost your confidence, and deepen your relationships. I have had many mentors over the years but there was a particular mentor that I had in my early twenties who had a big impact on my life. I am going to share that story with you and, in the process, I am going to break down five principles she really excelled at and taught to me.

1. Make introductions and teach

The thing about a good mentor is they build you up when you don't have confidence yet or when you suffer a blow in business that dings your confidence. When you're at the new stage where you still need to fake it till you make it because you don't believe it yet, they help you believe in yourself.

When I first met my mentor, Dianna, I was 26 years old and had a six-week-old baby at home. I had just gotten my first real, adult, post-education job. It was a government position, and I was super excited to be making a living wage and having benefits for the first time in my life. I was also overwhelmed, scared, and totally lacking in confidence. It was terrifying, I had all these responsibilities both at home and at work. There were so many things to learn. I was a civilian working on a military base with no idea of how the rank structure worked except what I had learned in movies.

I didn't know who to call "Sir" or "Ma'am" and who to refer to by their rank and who to call by their first name. There were acronyms for literally everything, including the buildings, and I had no idea what any of them stood for. I also had a new baby at home who was the joy of my life, but who kept me up late nights and required so much of my time, attention, and energy. So, I was distracted and suffering from postpartum anxiety. My hormones were raging and, honestly, I was kind of a mess even if it was not obvious to those on the outside.

But in all of this, I had this amazing lady who was one of my indirect supervisors. She took it upon herself to mentor me without being asked. She did the normal things a mentor would do like stop by my desk to see how things were going and let me know she was available if I had questions. But she went further than that also. She would schedule time in her day for us to talk about projects she was planning. She asked for my input, and she would walk me through problems that had come up and how she was resolving them.

She literally opened her brain and the inner workings of her job to me, and she did so with no fear of me trying to take over her job. She gave no thought to being too vulnerable by sharing challenges and asking for input. She was liked and respected by all her colleagues, and she took time to introduce me to all of them, even the Wing Commander at the top of the hierarchy. I learned from her how to treat the brand-new student employee.

She showed me that it was as important to treat newbies well as it was to take care of people high up in the chain of command. I watched her treat the cleaning staff with the same kindness, consideration, and interest as visiting officials. I watched her cultivate relationships everywhere she went with every conversation.

2. Build Confidence and show gratitude

I also learned about the value of giving positive feedback and recognizing other people's efforts. I'd be working away on a project for her. I would get so wrapped up in it that sometimes I would not look up to stop. Hours passed like minutes.

At the end of the day, I would go to leave and there beside my coat or by my purse would be a thank you card, a little note, maybe a little box of chocolate. She would leave something that said, "You are awesome! Keep up the good work! Could not have done it without you! Thank you!"

I didn't have it completely figured out what I needed to do yet, but she did such a great job of building my confidence that I wasn't afraid to take some risks here and there because I had such a safe place to land. She brilliantly bridged that gap between lack of knowledge about what I was doing and being confident that if I just tried my best, I could figure it out. That's one of the most valuable things a mentor can do for you — build your confidence and tell you when you are getting it right.

A great mentor will introduce you to other people who can help you. They will share their strategies with you and be your cheerleader and confidence builder. You know what else they do? They are also honest with you when they know you are capable of more and are underachieving. They are not afraid to push you harder or tell you to pull up your socks and focus.

3. Tell the truth even when its uncomfortable.

I had been working for a few years and let's just say the pace was not always grueling. Some days we were run off our feet and had to stay late to catch up. But just as often, there was time to grab a morning coffee and chat with coworkers. Sometimes people came in a few minutes late or took more than the allotted number of coffee breaks. Sometimes people left early for appointments and ran home midday to let a repairman in the house. Things seemed pretty relaxed, and I started to think that when in Rome perhaps I should do as the Romans do.

I started to take my time getting started in the mornings. I would take longer lunches and would wander down the hall to visit with coworkers more frequently. Do you think she let that slide? She sure didn't.

She called me on it, not because she was hard-nosed about the rules, but because she knew that when you start developing bad habits, you can carry them through the rest of your life.

She was not even my direct supervisor, but she could see what was happening and was worried about how it would affect my future opportunities.

One day, I was getting ready to take one of those extra breaks. She stopped me and asked me to come see her in her office. She looked at me for a few moments before she spoke.

"You know, you're not the same person you were two years ago when we first hired you, when you first started."

"What do you mean?" I asked. "Of course, I'm the same person. That's ridiculous."

She stood her ground. "No, you're not the same Monica. Instead of coming in at 7:30, you come in at 7:35. Sometimes you bring your breakfast and eat it at your desk before you start working. Sometimes you take an hour and fifteen minutes for lunch instead of an hour. You stand in the coffee room for 20 minutes chatting about your weekend."

I was shocked and embarrassed that she had noticed. I mean, everyone else did it all the time. What was the big deal? But she read my mind.

"Look," she said. "I know everyone else does it but you are not everyone else. Don't do what everyone else is doing. Do better. This doesn't affect me. You're getting your work done.

You can do whatever you want, but I am telling you if I see it, then other people see it too. It's going to affect your future employment opportunities. It's going to affect your ability to build trust and credibility with colleagues." She added, "Would you rather wait until someone else tells you when they hand you a pink slip?"

This was an eye opener for me, and it was uncomfortable to hear. But this is what good mentors do; they set the bar high, and they're not afraid to tell you when you have dropped it too low.

When you're screwing up and you need to pull up your socks and do something different, they call you out on it. They do so with honesty, grace, and kindness.

4. Encourage growth even when it represents a loss for you.

Do you know what else mentors do? They genuinely want to see you grow even if it means they lose you. When I told her I had seen a posting for another position at a higher rate of pay with more responsibility, she didn't waste time thinking about herself or how it would affect the projects I was working on for her. She said, "I think you are ready, let's talk about this."

Then she cleared her schedule and spent an hour with me talking about the pros and cons of what she knew about the position.

We talked about my motivations for wanting to move forward and whether this position would help me to grow in the areas where I wanted to grow.

She told me how to evaluate the job:

- Always look at more than just the pay.
- Will you be happy there?
- Will you have opportunities to grow further?
- Is it a good fit?"

After going through all the positives and negatives and talking about the changes I would need to make in my schedule and personal life if I got it, she told me to go update my resume and write a cover letter to bring back to her for review. Together, we went over my submission. We talked about possible questions that might come up, and she coached me on how to make the best possible first impression.

I put together my application, submitted it, and waited. When I got the call that I was being considered for the position, we again went over possible interview questions and possible answers. She told me what she knew about the people on the hiring committee, what she thought they were looking for, and why she thought I was a good fit.
Even as she was preparing me to spread my wings and fly away, she was still building my confidence.

The day of the interview finally came. I was so nervous, I was sitting at my desk distracted, trying to work, and sipping coffee. She stopped in front of my desk.

"What on earth are you doing? Isn't your interview today?"

"Yes," I said. "But don't worry. It's not for at least another 10 minutes. I have lots of time. I am just getting caught up on some work."

She gave her sternest look and in a voice that offered no argument she pointed at the door and said, "Get out of that chair, put down that coffee, get yourself a bottle of water, and go for a walk. You need to clear your head. You need to get your thoughts straight and you need to burn off some adrenaline or your nervousness is going to come through in that interview."

She was right. I did need to do all of those things. In fact, it was some of the best advice anyone ever gave me. Now when I need to do something important, or I must give a presentation with a clear head, I still heed her advice. I grab a bottle of water, and I go for a walk to burn off some adrenaline because that's what my body needs before I go into a stressful situation.

We kept in touch long after we worked at different companies and in different industries. She had one final lesson for me as a mentor years later:

5. Make time for life

She had worked hard for more than three decades when she finally retired.

Several of her colleagues planned a wonderful retirement party, and we enjoyed listening to her talk about all her plans for the future. She was going to go on cruises, throw amazing parties, and spend more time with her kids. She was going to do more dancing with her partner and try more new things. In fact, she was going to do all the things she didn't have time to do when she was working.

Not long after that, I ran into her downtown. She seemed to have to really think about who I was and what to say to me. I found out shortly after that that she had been diagnosed with Dementia. Before long, she didn't even know who I was. It progressed very quickly and not much longer after that she passed away. Her final lesson for me was that tomorrow isn't promised, so live fully present today. Be kind, extend grace, and do the things you love because you don't know what tomorrow brings. I will forever be grateful for the time and knowledge she shared with me and that I am now part of her legacy.

Seek out mentors and mentor others. No matter how early or advanced you are in your career or your business, there is always someone you can teach and someone you can learn from. Don't be afraid to share your knowledge and experience with someone, and don't be afraid to reach out and ask someone to mentor you. The worst thing that will happen is they will say no. But I bet they won't!

Be grateful for the introductions and the wisdom and the confidence a good mentor can give you and then give it away again to someone else. That mentor/mentee relationship is one of the most powerful relationships you will ever be a part of. Seek them out, they are worth it.

Never waste your mentor's time. Always show up five minutes before they expect you and leave when the meeting is over. If your mentor squeezes out an hour for you, don't take an hour and fifteen. They will be gracious and allow you to stay, but you should be equally gracious and leave. Also, let your mentor do the talking. You are the student. So, listen twice as much as you talk so that you can soak up as much of their knowledge as you can in the time they give you.

Notes

CHAPTER 18 - LEARNING TO LOVE YOURSELF

*"Accept yourself. Love yourself.
And keep moving forward. If you
want to fly, you have to give up
what weighs you down."*
~ Roy T. Bennett

As long as we are talking about advice and encouragement, who do you think you talk to most in a day? Is that your parents, your spouse, a sibling, a friend? Whatever answers you just came up with, I'm going to hazard a guess that they are all wrong. In fact, the person that you talk to the most every day is likely the person you look at in the mirror every morning.

Yes, that's *you* I am talking about.

You know how sometimes we talk to family members or loved ones more harshly than we would a total stranger. Well guess what? We talk to ourselves even more harshly than we do our loved ones. The conversations you have with yourself have more impact on your health, your wealth, and your emotional well being than any other conversation, yet most of us don't even give a second thought to our thoughts.

I don't know about you, but if I get on the scale in the morning and I weigh more than I expected, I immediately launch into a negative diatribe of "why did you have to eat _____ yesterday? I can't believe you haven't gone for a walk this week. You better get your act together."

On the other hand, if I have lost a few pounds the resulting conversation is not much better. It goes something like this. "Oh, wow I'm losing weight. I can treat myself to something special today.

Maybe I'll take a day off from the gym, I've earned it." Or perhaps you go in this direction: "Only a pound. See, you shouldn't have had that birthday cake at your cousin's party. It would be two pounds if you hadn't overeaten yesterday."

Our minds are powerful debaters and can talk us in or out of just about anything we want or don't want. In a split second, we can talk ourselves into bad decisions and out of good decisions with very little effort. How do we get around this? We change the conversation with ourselves. Think about it, we are the people we spend the most time around. Eventually we become more and more like the people we hang out with.

If the voice in your head is a negative one, that has a powerful, lasting effect on all areas of your life. What you say to yourself impacts your life and the outcomes in your day. There are a few different informal studies that support this. One of those studies was done on athletes, and the results are well-known. Athletes that engage in positive, outcome-based self-talk perform better, win more often, progress faster in training, and have more confidence.

[1]Researchers took a group of high jumpers and separated them into 2 groups. Group one engaged in non-specific self-talk. Such as, "You will do great today" or "you can do better today than yesterday."

As a result, they did perform better than previously, jumping higher or further and reporting greater feelings of confidence. They had more positive training experiences and looked forward to competitions more.

The second group engaged in self-talk, but it was much more specific and accompanied by videos showing them what techniques to visualize. For instance, instead of, "You got this; you are awesome," they were guided to say, "Jill you are going to crush this. You are going to jump 2 cm higher than last time. You are going to raise your hips and twist your torso as you go over the marker at the highest point in the jump." By giving themselves specific actionable criteria, they could see and visualize the outcome before they even started. [1]

This group outperformed the first group and exceeded their previous performance. Their brains took what they said, translated it, and instructed their body what to do.

This is powerful stuff in any area of life. Your self-talk is like a power pill. What you say to yourself and how you say it really matters in a tangible, measurable way.

Let's look at study number 2. There was this guy who was a psychologist named Ethan Kross. He gave 89 participants 5 minutes to draft a speech.

---

[1] J Sports Sci. 2008 Nov;26 (13):1459-65

He told half of them to use general pronouns like "you" and he told the other half to use their first names to address themselves while prepping and building their confidence[2].

The first half used language like "you can do this, you are a great speaker" while the second half used their names: "Bill you've got this, Bill you are going to crush it". Interestingly enough the group that used their first names had less anxiety, expressed more confidence and were perceived not only to perform better but to spend less time later worrying about the outcome.

He did more research on this and found out that when we talk to ourselves in the third person using our own names, we take ourselves more seriously. We're more likely to take action and to believe in ourselves. If this is true, then it's really important because it impacts us on a deep level. If we just say, "Oh, you're such an idiot," it kind of just rolls off us.

But, if I use my name and say, "Monica, you're such an idiot," that goes to my core. That's like someone else talking directly to me.

I applied this to my personal life. There was a time when I got on the scale in the morning and discovered that I weighed two pounds more even though I ate less all week, and I would say, "Monica, you can never lose this weight. Just give up."

---

[2] [2] Forbes Feb 2 2021, Bryan Robinson Phd

My body took that and internalized it. It became part of my belief system about myself. It held me back from doing the things that I really want to do and from succeeding in areas that challenged me.

Now I speak powerfully and impactfully to myself. I want to really hear it and internalize it. So, I use my first name.

Instead of, "Monica, you will never lose the weight," I could say, "Monica, you are doing all the right things. Keep up the great work! Change takes time!" The more I did this, the greater my results. In the last year, I have slowly lost 20 lbs a little at a time. Have I done other things? Yes. Have I connected with likeminded people who support me? Yes. Have I changed my choices? Definitely!

But ultimately, I have also changed the internal dialogue of the way I talk to myself. When I look in the mirror now, I say aloud, "You are a rockstar, Monica. You are going to have a great day." Or "Monica, it's a beautiful day to help someone grow. Who are you going to be kind to today?" This changes how I think about myself and others and it's a powerful tool to have in your tool kit. Remember our discussion of rewiring the brain? This is one of the most effective ways to do it. I am breaking down those negative lines and building positive superhighways that make it easy to love and believe in myself. I am crushing self-doubt and feeding my faith in my abilities.

If I am getting up to say a speech and I'm feeling nervous or unsure, or if I'm worried that I'm going to forget stuff, I could say, "OMG! I am so nervous I am going to forget everything," or I could make it worse by saying, "Monica, you are so nervous, how will you remember anything?

Instead, I choose to flip the conversation and make it a valuable one — one that is specific and supports me as it increases my confidence. I say, "Monica, you got this. You are going to remember everything. You are going to speak in a calm level voice that is easy to understand. You are going to make eye contact with your audience and share your passion for this subject with them. You are powerful, you are a great speaker. I can't wait to hear the recording later"

The amount of time we spend talking to ourselves is shocking. We literally talk to ourselves nonstop all day long. Even when we don't realize we're doing it, we're doing it. What we need to do is, when we catch ourselves, control that conversation. Immediately, we must say something empowering to ourselves.
Think about when you're in a conversation with someone and the other person just keeps talking over you and interrupting you. You find yourself up against this wall of negativity. If that's what you are doing to yourself, stop now!

When thoughts come up that don't serve me, I say, "shut the cluck up." Yes, I really say, "SHUT THE CLUCK UP." (OK, I might sometimes use an expletive that's not "cluck," but you get the point).

Then I refocus the conversation to something positive. I find gratitude, and I point it out to myself because my brain likes evidence. Gratitude is a type of evidence that supports a different thought pattern. It's a great way to build new and better neural pathways.

For example, last year my friend's RV pump failed. The week before, she had an issue with the RV lights. Both times the problems came up, I was nearby and was able to troubleshoot and solve the problem with her. I was amazed though at how quickly she went straight into negative talk. "I have the worst luck. Everything bad happens to me. These things come in threes, so something else will be coming soon."

If my inner voice started on that, I would tell it to SHUT THE CLUCK UP! So, I decided to share my positive outlook with her.

"What are you talking about?" I asked. "Think about how lucky you are."

She looked at me as if I was crazy. "What are you talking about? I have horrible luck. Everything bad happens to me."

"Well for one thing, when you had an electrical issue, you had an extended warranty and the guy had a cancellation and was able to come out the same day.

He fixed it in about 10 minutes and while he was here, he fixed another problem for no extra charge. That seems pretty lucky to me."

She didn't really know what to say to that, so she tried to wiggle over to another problem. "Well, my septic pump just broke."

"Yes, and isn't it great I was home and I could come and help you disconnect it, pick up a new one, and help you hook it up. Isn't it great that your neighbor let you use her bathroom and her shower and that you didn't have to go into the woods? Don't forget the new pump is even better than the old one, and it was on sale today. If it had broken tomorrow, the sale would be over. It would have cost more and your neighbor would have been at work with the door locked so you couldn't use her bathroom. Also, it's a beautiful sunny day to be out here putting in a new pump. It's not cold, raining, or snowing. Seems pretty lucky to me."

She knew she was beaten. "Well, I never thought of it that way. I guess I am pretty lucky!"

She has never thought of it that way because she had never been intentional with her thoughts. She just let her reptilian mind run wild inventing reasons to complain. She accepted the negative reality as true just because they popped into her head not knowing they were harmful to her mental wellbeing. Her thoughts left her feeling bad and affected her in so many other ways.

Those negative voices (negative neural pathways) kept her from applying for a job she wanted because she told herself she would never get the job due to her lack of qualifications.

Negativity kept her from finding a partner because she convinced herself she wasn't pretty enough or was too old. The list of things her negative superhighway stole from her is endless.

How do we change our thoughts?

I'll tell you what I do and you can decide if it works for you or not. First of all, I became aware.
Awareness is the critical step that sets all good things in motion. Just being aware of the fact that I have an internal voice is huge. Most of us are not even aware of how much time we spend in conversation with ourselves.

To break the cycle of negative thoughts, we start by being intentional with our words. No longer do we just open our mouths and let anything come out. We are careful with our spoken words which helps us to be careful with our internal words.
And we start the process of being careful with our words at the beginning of the day when we wake. We start with positivity: "This is going to be a great day _____ (insert name here), I am so excited."

For me, there are so many opportunities to shift the internal conversation in a day. When I arrive at work and I find out that a file I have been working on for weeks has fallen through, instead of retreating to that negative highway and saying, "Oh great! I did all that work for nothing," I choose to say, "Well, I am glad I found out now instead of two weeks from now when I had even more time into it. What a great learning experience that was. Let me think about what I can do to prevent that again in the future."

212

That immediately kicks my brain into creative and grateful mode — grateful for the opportunity to tweak the way I do things and creatively thinking of how I can change my process so it doesn't happen again.

In one case, the client got a better offer from their bank. In reviewing the file, I realized that I had access to that same bank. If I had just asked them at the beginning if they had an interest in staying with their own bank, I could have uncovered that I could have gotten them a mortgage there, which would have prevented them from going back to their bank in the first place.

I was not dejected. I was excited. I learned something and have a new process that will save me time and lost files. It was great — a win for everyone. I was glad I figured it out on a small file so I could have a new process in place for a bigger file. I said to myself, "Brilliant! This is awesome! Great, Monica!"

The moral of this story? If you are going to criticize yourself, don't use your first name. You might even give yourself a made-up name and alter ego to blame everything on so it doesn't feel like you are talking to yourself. Instead of Monica, I might blame Maggie and say, "Oh, Maggie, you goose. You are so clumsy. Next time, let Monica handle it! She's awesome!"

Notice the negative talk and reframe it. You can also set your day up for success by finding gratitude in everything. The more we notice what is working the more things work out.

As you become more careful with your speech, also consider being careful about who you allow to speak to you. We are the sum of thoughts we allow to take up space in our minds. But in that mix are the people we hang out with most. If we surround ourselves with people who are consistently negative, we are more likely to sink into complaining and ungratefulness. Misery loves company. People who insist on being miserable will not abide by your positive, upbeat nature. They will try to drag you down with them. And, even worse than hanging out with negative people who put themselves down is spending time with people who put you down. If your inner circle doesn't support you, cheer you, and celebrate your wins, they don't belong in your inner circle.

Everything you say to yourself and what others say to you goes deep into your subconscious and help to form or destroy neural pathways. How you talk to yourself is like exercising a muscle; the more you do it the stronger and more developed it gets. Speaking like a winner leads to thinking like a winner. Thinking like a winner leads to acting like a winner, which leads to taking actions that lead to winning.

You can't control how other people talk to you (except to keep away from them), but you can control how YOU talk to YOU. Choose your words with care because they have a direct impact on your success.

Notes

CHAPTER 19 - NO MEANS NO

"It is necessary and even vital to set standards for your life and the people you allow in it."
~ Mandy Hale

In the early 21st century, women who had been sexually abused or harassed found their strength. They began to speak up. Many of them finally saw their abusers take their places behind prison walls. A hashtag began to circulate: #metoo. It symbolized that woman had the right to say no to any sexual advance. It was a great time of liberation.

It is a critical human right — the right to say no. But far too often, we allow obligation, fear, or the threat of loss to keep us from saying no to someone who deserves to hear no.

Picture this. It's 8pm on a Friday night, and my client is texting me. As I click on the talk button on my phone, I feel a knot in my stomach because I'm supposed to be watching a movie with my kids. But I don't know how to not answer. It seems rude and violates my philosophy of stellar customer service. It happens all the time with all kinds of clients. They love that I am always available. I hate that I am ALWAYS available.

Even before she said one word, I was asking myself, "Why is this client texting me at 8pm. How does my being available right now add value to the transaction for me or her? I'm not at my desk. I don't have her file. I already checked in with her yesterday with an update and promised to call her again Monday. What can I possibly do at this hour of the day?" Most times nothing can be solved at that time. If there is a problem, it likely can't be dealt with until the morning. If it's a question, it can probably wait until the next business day at a respectable hour.

Sure, I could have said, "I'll get back to you in the morning." But the question or problem is still going to hang over my evening. I will be distracted by it and, eventually, it's going to have an effect on my sleep, quality of my life, and the quality of my other relationships.

Here is the thing it took me years to learn. *I taught this client to do this. I taught this client that I work 24/7.* The first time I let it happen, I trained her to call whenever she had the urge. I failed to set boundaries and, therefore, created a monster.

Can you blame me? It's tough to say no. When you love to take good care of your clients, you want to be there for them as much as possible. But when your professional responsibility interferes with the rest of your life, you have to draw some lines. What if a client gets a sudden thought at midnight about their deal? Is it acceptable for them to pick up the phone and call you or wake you from a sound sleep with a text alert? Of course not.

Believe it or not, you can actually say no without saying no, and you can do it without your client actually realizing it. The language we use, the phrases that we choose, and the way we say them, help with how our message is perceived. You can set boundaries with clients without them actually being aware that we are even setting them. If you do it right, you will find that it strengthens relationships instead of creating tension and resentment.

That first time she texted me outside of office hours and I responded right away without saying anything about the time, I taught her that it was acceptable. My inaction set up the chain of texts and calls that followed. First, she texted me in the evening, then she started texting me in the early morning house, and then she started texting me on the weekends.

I really didn't mind the first time. It was just one question. It was an answer I knew and could deliver quickly before saying goodbye. I really didn't mind. But before I knew it, it started to become a regular thing and it started to create this festering resentment that seeped into the rest of my life.

I started to get annoyed and resentful. I started to blame Mrs. Brown for being so inconsiderate. I'd pick up my phone and think, "I can't believe this woman is texting me on a Saturday afternoon. How rude! Does she not realize I have a family? Does she not realize that I have a life?"

I am certain my frustration would come through in my tone. She couldn't see my eye rolling, but I am certain she could feel it.

Decades ago, State Farm Insurance Company was the number one insurance provider and had a high customer service rating. Back then, their customer service philosophy was based on one phrase, "Put a smile in your voice."

Agents were trained to smile because they believed customers could "see" it even though they were talking on the phone. They were right. Humans are acutely tuned in. Even if the words are perfect, we can pick up on subtle changes in tone.

Mrs. Brown couldn't see on the other end of the line and deep, silent sighs I let out because I allowed myself to get dragged into a conversation that could have totally waited until Monday morning. Inside I would be fuming and wondering what was wrong with her? But really, it was on me. I taught her that it was okay to text me at any time.

I didn't specifically phone her up and say, "Mrs. Brown, I am available 24/ 7. You can text me, call me, email me, Facebook message me at any hour of any day. You can reach me however you want, whenever you want." No, I didn't say it in that many words. I just said nothing when she did it and immediately responded with an answer.

My own inaction and unwillingness to gently set a boundary also set the clear expectation that it's okay for her to text me whenever a question pops into her head. And why wouldn't she? It's human nature — you have a question, you ask it. It's so convenient, and that kind of responsiveness is a huge asset that <u>can</u> set you apart from your competitors. *That is until it doesn't* because you are burnt out and resentful and you can't give your clients the attention they deserve during work hours because you are always in work mode. Remember, we are in the long game. We are farmers, not hunters.

I would learn a lot from all those types of clients that routinely crossed the line. In fact, I would eventually get annoyed enough to respond with a request not to text or call on evenings or weekends. I have had to have some uncomfortable conversations that went a little like this: "Evenings and weekends are my family time, and this is my personal cell phone. I would appreciate it if you would only contact me within business hours."

Interestingly enough, people didn't think that was a very nice response. They thought it was quite rude actually. It made people feel bad and in return they got offended they associated me with making them feel that way. It was bad for relationships. I had to find a better way to make my point without alienating my customers.

It was really a bit of a bait and switch on my part if you think about it. I led them to believe that it was perfectly okay to call me anytime. Then I lashed out and reprimanded them, making them feel bad. I made them feel like a little kid getting in trouble or like they had broken an unspoken social rule and been called out on it. My tone and my abruptness made them feel embarrassed, and when we make clients feel embarrassed or awkward, they associate us with those feelings and don't want to come back.

Maya Angelo once said:

> *"People will forget what you said,*
> *but they will never forget how we*
> *made them feel."*

What if I backed all the way up to the first time I met Mrs. Brown and reframed how she could contact me in a positive way? Instead of saying, "don't call me on weekends or evenings," which is a "no" phrase, I could say, "I am happy to answer any and all questions that come up, please email me anytime, and I will call you back as soon as I am in the office." I would give her my standard office hours and then set my auto reply each day so that she knew when she could expect to hear back from me. In that way, I would be telling her no, but I would be doing it in a positive way.

Some customers don't get the hint and will bypass email, opting rather to texts in the evening? I can simply reply with a text that reads:

"Thanks so much for reaching out.
I'll call you or email you in the
morning when I'm at the office"
or
"Great Question! Could you send
this in an email so I can look at it
first thing when I get to the office
on Monday?"

It's all about the presentation. These phrases frame the response positively.

There's any number of things that I could have said that would have set the tone for the future while saying yes instead of no.

"Here's the answer you need for
tonight. It's quite lucky that I saw

your text because I don't usually check my texts in the evening as that is my family time. It's best to email me for a quick response as soon as I get to the office in the morning."

By setting expectations at the first meeting and responding with a "yes" boundary statement, I can ensure that there are never any hurt feelings or the sense of abandonment when I don't respond outside of my working hours.

Going back to the communications discussion, remember to always let the customer know that they are going to have impromptu questions. But also let them know that you will be routinely following up:

"I know that questions are going to come up along the way, and I am here to answer them for you. I prefer email so that I have a record of everything we talked about to refer back to, but if you need a call back. just drop me a note and I will get back to you right away with a time to chat."

or

"Please write down your questions as they arise, and I will do my best to get answers for you as quickly as you can. If you have something truly urgent, then go ahead and call. But weekends and evenings

are for my family time, and I would appreciate it if you could save routine questions for weekdays when I am fresh and can give you my full attention and have answers available to me."

Or

"If you text me or email me on the weekend, you may not get an immediate response, but the reality is there's almost nothing I can do on the weekends. Lenders are closed. Banks are closed. I can't access the information that I need. If you send me an email over the weekend, I will respond first thing when I'm back in the office. I really appreciate it."

You might be working in an industry where it's totally normal to call and text at all hours of the day and weekend. Maybe you are a real estate agent and you want people to call you on the weekend because Saturdays and Sundays are great days to visit properties or check out Open Houses.

If that's the case, then tell them that too so they know it's ok. The point is they can't read your mind; if you don't tell them what's ok and what's not, they really don't know.

With Mrs. Brown, there are a lot of different things I could have said to set the tone, set the expectation, and lay the groundwork for her, so that she knew in a positive way what the expectation was. Had I done that, the first text would've probably been the last text from her going forward. I am certain she would have respected my time. In fact, she might have had more respect for me for laying that boundary than letting her walk all over me and then getting annoyed.

Last week I had someone reach out to me with something that was somewhat urgent. I needed to craft the best "yes" response I could:
"Hey! I really appreciate that this answer is important and time sensitive. So, I'm giving you a quick call back so we can sort this out tonight. But I just want you to know for the future that this is an exception. I don't normally take calls in the evening. That's my family time."

The client was completely understanding. "Wow!" he said. "Of course, I should know that someone as busy as you would have set hours so you can be efficient." He was quite happy to get the information he needed and also knew that he was being given an exception because it was important. But if you don't tell your clients the truth because you're afraid of hurting their feelings or because you're afraid of not seeming like you're doing a good enough job, you're actually setting yourself up for failure. You unintentionally create a habit and a set of expectations.

When you do it for one person, you will do it for the next person, and pretty soon word gets out that you are available 24/7. Before you know it, you're responding to requests all night, all day long, every weekend, leaving you with little time for yourself and the ones you love. You will build resentment for your clients. In time, you will start to burn out and find that you are not as fresh and motivated as you could be. All the parts of your life get mixed together and you find yourself trying to do personal things on work time and vice versa. You will lose the joy of your work and find yourself easing your way out of the business.

You may find that a client wants or needs a weekend appointment. What should you do if you don't work weekends? You could say, "No, I don't work weekends." But that would be a negative or "no" response. Instead, you could say "Yes, of course. You should know that there is never a charge for appointments during the week. But there is a $200 call-in fee for weekends because that's my personal time." Now you've attached a price tag to it and made your time a valuable commodity. If it's worth it to them, then great. You'll go and you'll get paid for your time.

If it's not worth it to you, don't dangle that carrot. But it is a way of saying yes instead of saying no.

Notes

CHAPTER 20 - PEOPLE RISE TO THE EXPECTATION YOU SET

"There is no greater power and support you can give someone than to look them in the eye, and with sincerity and conviction, say, 'I believe in you.'"
~ Ken Poirot

Human beings place great value in what other human beings think of them. If you can tunnel this truth deep in your mind and let it guide your working philosophy, you will find it easier to manage your work week.

Try this technique in your daily operations. For instance, instead of saying, "I'm sorry for asking for so many documents," you can say shift the conversation. You could say, "Thank you for being so responsive and getting me all of the documents quickly." Now the reality may be that the client is not responsive at all, and complains about every document you ask for. But once you start thanking them for the behavior you want, they actually try to earn your praise. This is basic human psychology.

Never apologize every time you ask for a document. You place a negative stamp on the process when you do like it's something you should be apologizing for. Flip the conversation instead, and say:
Thank you for the documents that you've provided. Thank you for being so responsive. It's great to work with someone who's so prompt about returning things to me.

If you point out someone's defects, those defects will get worse. If you praise the behavior you wish to see, you will eventually see it. Try this on someone in your life who is chronically late. Praise them for working so hard to be on time even if they showed up late. You will find that it helps them to be more on time.

When you make people feel awesome, they want to continue to be awesome in your eyes. They want to live up to that expectation.

My clients are so respectful of my time. I've got amazing clients that are really careful about not contacting me on my personal time unless it's an emergency. And that way, if the phone rings and it's a client, I know it's something I should pick up because it's a genuine emergency.

If you are the person that's constantly telling someone what a crappy job they did, they will always feel like they can't measure up. If you're pointing out their flaws and criticizing them, they will stop trying to perform at a higher level. Be careful that you are not telling people everything they did wrong. They will start to avoid you. They will do everything they can to not have to work with you. And they will lower the bar low enough that they think they can reach it.

In other words, bad behaviour will get worse and worse and worse.
As humans, we thrive on affirmation. So, if there are things that you like about what they're doing, tell them repeatedly. If there is nothing, find something or make something up.

When I first get a mortgage application, I put all the information together and then I send it to someone called an underwriter.

It's essentially the underwriter's job to review all the documents, pick them apart, and make a decision about whether or not to approve the file. And as a mortgage broker, the relationship that I have with those underwriters is important. It's probably one of the most important relationships that I have.

It's even more important than the relationship that I have with my clients, because it's the difference between getting a file approved quickly and getting a file approved slowly. It's the difference between them picking up my deal right away or leaving my file to rot on a never-ending pile of files they have to work with. I work to be someone who is easy to work with. I like to talk through a problem rather than present myself as someone who creates problems.

If underwriters decide they don't like someone's income or they want an extra document or they're too busy, they can make your life a living hell. They can just say no to the application or take forever to say yes.

When I was just starting at a new company, I'd been assigned an underwriter that everyone hated. Everyone said, "Oh no, you've got her. She's horrible. She's a nightmare. She rewrites your whole file. She changes everything. She asks for the stupidest documents. She'll argue with you about everything. She doesn't understand the rules. She's a total control freak. She's a power tripper."

I was terrified to work with her. But I said, "Well, let me go into this with an open mind. Let me see how bad she really is. I'm going to form my own opinions about her." I honestly had never met an underwriter that I didn't like and couldn't get along with. So, I was really surprised at the comments being made about her. I can form relationships with people that other people struggle with.

I thought, "No, she can't be as bad as everyone says. It's not going to be that difficult." Wow, was I ever wrong. It <u>was</u> that difficult. She was argumentative. She picked apart my file. She brought up every rule in the book to see how she was going to apply it. Everything I asked for, she said no. Every exception I asked for, she denied. Every document I sent her, she rejected. It was a freaking nightmare.

I thought, "Ok, I can do one of two things. I can continue to work with her and we can push each other back and forth and have pissing contests all day. We can fight over who is going to control this file, and I can hate every moment of working with her. I can complain to her manager about her. I can fight her on everything.

Or, I can focus on what *was* working.

Usually, it's pretty easy for me to find a couple of things that I like about someone and tell them what they are. Usually, when I share with them what those good things are, it takes them off guard.

As human beings, we like praise but rarely hear it. We like for people to tell us what we do well and know how hard we are trying.

We want to live up to people's expectations. If someone tells me I am the best mortgage broker they've ever had and that I'm awesome. I will go to any lengths to make sure that they continue to feel that way forever. If, on the other hand, someone tells me I did a crappy job and they're not happy with it, I have a hard time trying to prove why they are wrong.

Most people, when they hear how awful they are, think "Oh well, she thinks I'm a piece of crap anyway. So, who cares?"

We all have egos, and I have never met an ego that didn't like to be stroked. So, what we need to do is leverage those egos honestly and authentically. I thought about how I could win this woman to my side. I thought I should write a "high five" review for her. I positioned my fingers over the keys as I sat there and stared at the screen. I thought, "Oh my gosh, I can't even think of one nice thing to say about this person. What am I going to write? And for a minute, I actually thought about emailing her manager and telling him what a crappy job she did, how difficult it was to work with her.

I thought they needed to provide her some training on how to be a good underwriter. And then it came to me. I realized that there was something she'd been exceptionally good at.

She was responsive every single time I sent her an email. She responded back to me every time I phoned her. She was not always pleasant. But she was prompt and responsive.

Even though she was cranky, argumentative, and wrapped up in her own idea of things, she got one thing right. That thought led me to another thought. She also had advice for me when she responded. It wasn't always the advice that I wanted to hear. She would tell me how she thought I should get the file done. While I did not appreciate someone else telling me how to do my job, the reality is that the file got approved when I did it her way because of the feedback that she gave me.

She never gave me the warm fuzzies or wrapped up her comments in a bow, but she did give me feedback. And when I applied that feedback, my file closed successfully.

I chose to ignore everything that I didn't like about her — everything that was bothering me about her manner. I chose to focus on those two things and wrote a review. I said:

"Thank you for always being so responsive. You answered every email. You picked up every phone call immediately, and that helped.

And your feedback was helpful for me to learn how to get challenging files done. I appreciate how responsive you were and your feedback was valuable."

I didn't lie. I didn't say it was pleasant to work with her. I simply focused on what I could say truthfully. I cc'd her manager. An hour later, she called me nearly in tears and said, "Thank you so much. No one has ever given me positive feedback. Everyone is always jumping down my throat. I really appreciate that. You took the time to do that and you made my day."

You can probably guess the rest of the story. From that day forward, our relationship completely transformed. She became easy to talk to and work with. She still gave me feedback, but she delivered it in a way that was open and transparent. She talked to me more like a coach than a dictator. She worked hard to get my files done for me quickly.

She even occasionally laughed and joked with me. I was getting to know who she was as a person. By the time she left to retire, she was one of my favorite underwriters. I always remembered to find something good to tell her about what she was doing. The more things I found, the more she rose to meet my expectations of her.

When you're confronted with someone who is difficult, try building a relationship with them using the materials you have.

Get them on your team so that you can work together. It may be really hard to find what they're doing right because there are a hundred things they're doing wrong. But I promise you there is always something. You just have to find it. Once you do, thank them for it. You will reap those rewards.

Notes

CHAPTER 21 - NETWORKING = VULNERABILITY

"Owning our own story can be hard, but not nearly as difficult as spending our lives running from it. Embracing our vulnerabilities is risky, but not nearly as dangerous as giving up on love, belonging, and joy — the experiences that make us the most vulnerable. Only when we are brave enough to explore the darkness will we discover the infinite power of life.
~ Brene Brown

There is only thing that can make your authentic self unappealing: being a jerk. If you are not sure if you are a jerk, you might take the advice I heard someone give. She said, "If you meet three jerks in a day, you are, in fact, the jerk." And it's true because I used to be that person. I used to walk through life thinking, "Oh my gosh, that guy's such an idiot. Why would he talk to me like that? Or I can't believe they screwed up my order. What a jerk, so rude." I would get home at the end of day and go through my list of all these people that were just horrible. In reality it was my own responses to things that made me the horrible one.

Now that doesn't happen to me very often anymore because I give all people grace, kindness, and patience. I understand that we are all just doing our best to make our way through the world. Every person alive craves love and acceptance. Now when I get up to the drive through where they screwed up my order, I don't freak out. I say, "No worries. You're all busy. I'll just pull over here and I'll wait. No problem." Or when I show up for my appointment and they're 20 minutes late, I say, "No big deal. I'll get some emails done." People notice when you extend grace to them since it's a rare gift these days.

I have another business inside a large veterinary hospital to satisfy my love of animals and desire to be around them. I am a canine reproduction technician/consultant there.

I can tell you that the staff notices the people that are not kind to them.

And the people who are, the people who extend grace stand head and shoulders above the people that lose their crap over every little thing that doesn't go their way.

In fact, many of the clients who bring their pets to the animal hospital are people who own businesses. They are realtors and massage therapists and couriers and sales professionals. What they don't realize is that their interactions with staff directly reflect on their businesses. When one of the staff members is looking to buy a new car or get a house or make a big purchase, they discuss which client's business to patronize.

Conversations go like this:

"What about Susan? She seems like a really busy realtor and her houses always have sold signs on them."

"No way, don't use her! Last time her prescription was wrong, she practically threw it back in my face. She is always nice to the doctor but super rude to the receptionists."

or

"You should use Anne. She is so patient and nice even when we are short staffed and running late. Remember she even brought us lunch that time her dog was sick and we had to work through lunch to take care of it"

Every day, people make decisions about who to do business with based on how those people make them feel, how they treat them and their staff, and how they interact in the world.

Be the nice person. Be the patient one. Don't be a jerk. If authentic you is a jerk then ask yourself why that is and what you can do to change it because it will not serve you or your business to continue that behaviour.

Be the person other people want to
do business with.

Some business owners are just jerks. But others are stressed because business is slow, staffing is challenging, or they have lost their love of the business. Perhaps they have a personal problem at home that they wish they could spend more time dealing with like a marital issue, sick child, or aging parents who need them, but they can't devote any time to that with a business that consumes every waking moment. They aren't necessarily jerks. They are just stressed out of their minds.

We can't change what's going on in their life or how they speak to us, but we can choose how we respond and whether or not we allow that one interaction to pollute the rest of our day. Remember you never know what's going on in someone's life; choose kindness even when it's not given to you. Often, how you react to a situation sets the tone for how the other person reacts also. Choose your words and your tone wisely.

One of the ways that we actually best connect with other human beings is through vulnerability. It is one of the reasons people don't connect: they fear being vulnerable. I understand. No one wants to be hurt. No one wants to appear weak. And no one wants to be seen as a failure. So, when people ask, "How's business?" We lie. Our first response, prompted by our reptile brain, is "Fine!" We think that we should act strong. We should pretend that everything's good, even when it's not. Most people, when you ask how their business is going, will answer, "Awesome. It's great. Never been busier."

What if we could tell the truth and be authentic? What if we could be vulnerable enough to ask for help? What if we could honestly respond, "I'm struggling a bit, or I'm facing a challenge with _____ I'd love some advise on how to move forward"

But we never say such things because it almost feels like there's an invisible wall between you and them. The truth is that there is. It is the desire to present a version of ourselves that is at least confident and at best, perfect.

We want people to think our lives are amazing. Nothing ever goes wrong. We have the answers to all the questions and don't need help. That builds a wall between people and it makes it really difficult for other people to connect with us.

That is why small groups of like-minded people are so important and effective. I highly recommend joining a mastermind group or creating your own. Find or create a place for like-minded people get together and share. Give each other strength and hope. Talk about real life. Wherever you find that group, keep looking if you have not found it yet. Find your tribe, it's out there.

We all need that place where we can share our own experiences and connect in our commonalities. In those environments, it becomes easier to be vulnerable because you know that others in the group have similar experiences and they are sharing just as much as you are. Chances are when you share your story, when you share what's troubling, when you share what you were struggling with, there are other people who are struggling with the same thing. They will encourage you and tell you what they did to overcome their struggles.

And guess what? You will help others as well. There are other people who will hear themselves in your story, who will connect with you on a human level. They need to hear from you just as much as you need to hear from them. They will help you to come to know and value your authentic self.

Imagine for a minute that you're in a room with a bunch of people. Everyone is nice. But there is that one guy…

There is one in every group. You know that guy — that person who's cocky and arrogant and knows everything.

He's the loud talker who interrupts people and finishes their sentences for them. Nobody believes a word he says. He is not someone you want to go up and talk to. And you would never want to ask his advice. You certainly would not want to do business with him.

That's the mindset you adopt when you feel obligated to give all the right answers like "Life is perfect. My life is great." Don't succumb to the urge to mask your security with overconfidence.

Be that person who is unafraid to just be. That is the person in the room we love to talk to. They are not wrapped in body armor. They don't have themselves encased in plexiglass. They are open and will let you in just a little bit.

Never be afraid to knock on the door of someone older, wiser, and more successful and say those five magic words: "Do you have a minute?"

When you are new in any industry, you are going to feel lost. To be honest, if you take my advice to act as if (which is great advice, by the way), you are going to feel like a fraud. There will be some days you won't even know what you're doing. That is what being vulnerable is all about.

People respond well to vulnerability because it is so authentic. Don't believe me?

Think about the last time you saw someone let their guard down and show who they really are? Did that make you want to connect with that person? When someone comes to me with their vulnerability out in the open and says, "Listen, this is where I'm struggling. I need some help as a fellow human being," I am all over it.

If it's within my capability, I want to help. It makes me want to get to know them and help them. It makes me want to connect. It makes me want to support them and elevate them. I see myself in them because I've been vulnerable. So, I create a safe place for them to be themselves.

I'm not a perfect person. I'm a human, just like them. And that makes me approachable. So I've had people just message me out of the blue and say, "Hey, I've been following you on social media. I met you at a conference, whatever. And I was wondering if you could… "

Sometimes they just want a few moments of my time to chat so they can pick my brain. When people tell me, "I'd just like to get your advice on some stuff that I just feel like I don't have a good handle on, and you seem like someone really, you seem really kind," to me, that is the biggest compliment in the world.

Who doesn't want to watch someone else grow? Who doesn't want to be asked for their advice? And when you make yourself vulnerable, you take down those walls. It's like, you're letting people in so they can see the real you. It is the greatest gift we can give each other as human beings.

Perhaps you remember the movie *Avatar*. The mantra of the alien tribe was "I see you." What they were trying to convey was that every person was unique and special in his or her own right. We are not nameless, faceless masses.

We are individual people with our own unique story, unique pain, and unique destinies. We want to be seen. Even the shyest among us who take their place on the wall at parties hoping to melt into the wallpaper does so because they want permission to be seen for who they really are.

Let's use an analogy for a minute. Pretend your life is a city. To stay safe, you may be tempted to place large and impenetrable walls around you. You may even construct a moat and a drawbridge and then station your army all around it to keep people out. You are hoping to keep your enemies out. That's a smart move. Enemies want nothing more than to break down those walls, pillage the city. The only problem is that no one can get in either.

In your attempt to protect yourself from hurt and ensure that you are safe, you have kept out the blessings that might come your way.

You shut out the good people like other merchants and traders, family from afar, and people you want to do business with and interact. Everyone is kept back when the bridge is pulled up. The opposite is also true that when the bridge is down, everyone can get in. That's the essence of vulnerability. That's the essence of being your authentic self. You could get hurt, <u>or</u> you could grow and thrive.

If you've got these walls up, consider lowering them even if only for a short time. Give yourself permission to be vulnerable. Sometimes, when people see that vulnerable side of you, they see themselves. And I guarantee you, if you're sharing something that you're struggling with, someone else is struggling with the same thing.

I used to lament that others are so outgoing and I suffer with the burden of being an introvert. I felt so alone until I got vulnerable enough to say "Hey, I'm a total introvert. Would all the other introverted people please come forward?"

Before I knew it. I was surrounded by a group of people who are just like me. I was not alone. There are plenty of people I can have a conversation with, and that I can connect to. Our weaknesses can be our strengths if we embrace them instead of running from them.

Let me illustrate this with a story. When I first started out in this industry, I won a trip to a huge national conference. I was so excited. I submitted the entry. I got the notification.

My trip was paid, all expenses, hotel, airfare, everything. I was like, "Oh, my gosh, this is so awesome." And then the day before I was supposed to go, I started freaking out and melting down. The reality of it hit me. I was going to a new place where I didn't know anybody.

I would be walking around, trying to make small talk with strangers all day. I mean, I knew when I went into workshops and speeches that I could sit there and listen, but then all of a sudden, I realized that I had to eat breakfast, lunch, and dinner and it would be so weird to sit all by myself or sit with strangers. There would be a trade show where I would have to walk around and talk to people. I was paralyzed with fear.

I wanted to cancel my trip, but I knew that I couldn't because someone else had paid for my plane tickets and my reservations. I decided I would go and sit in my workshops and then run back to my hotel room to hide.

Then it hit me that, if I was feeling this way, other people were probably feeling the same way. That is when I remembered that someone told me vulnerability is really strength and that vulnerability could be a connection with other people. So, I put on my big girl pants and I went onto one of our industry social media forums.

I made a little post that changed everything for me. I wrote:

> *"Listen, I won this trip. I'm going to the conference. And I got to be totally honest. I'm freaking out because I don't know anybody there. And I got some social anxiety. I'm a total introvert. If there's anyone else going who doesn't know anybody, who's totally alone, who's feeling like I am,*

*please reach out to me. Maybe we
can go for dinner. Maybe we can
keep each other company."*

Well, I kid you not, not less than 15 women reached out to me. They responded to my call. They said, "Hey, I'm also scared. Hey, I don't know anybody either." It turns out there were a lot of people having the same fears as me. And if I hadn't been brave enough to be vulnerable, I wouldn't have found that out. I connected with those women. We ate our meals together and attended our seminars together. We had a blast!

We even took a trip over to the casino together. I made friendships with those women that I will have for the rest of my life. And I did that by being a little bit vulnerable by putting myself out there and not being afraid.

So, get out there! Be kind, be vulnerable, plant seeds, help others, be of service and just keep putting one foot in front of the other, one connection, one transaction at a time. And tell me how it goes, I am cheering for you. You got this!

Notes

ABOUT THE AUTHOR

Monica Parkin is a licensed mortgage broker and successful serial entrepreneur. She is an award-winning international speaker and the host of the "Juggling without Balls" Podcast. She is also a self professed introvert and crazy goat lady who lives on a small farm with an assortment of furry creatures. She loves to hear feedback from readers and looks forward to opportunities to speak on topics that empower others to feel more connected, confident, and successful.

If you enjoyed this book, please leave a review where you purchased it to help others find it! Thank you

Printed in Great Britain
by Amazon